COHERENCE UNIVERSALISM

COHERENCE UNIVERSALISM

Social Dynamics

Institutions, Civilizations, and the Coherence Crisis of Modernity

Gaura Kiśora Dās Rader

Heaven≡Earth Press

Coherence Universalism Series • March 2026

Published by Heaven≡Earth Press
Athens, Ohio

Coherence Universalism Series

ISBN: 978-X-XXXX-XXXX-X (paperback)

This work is part of the Coherence Universalism framework. For the complete series and supporting materials, visit heavenearthfoundation.org.

Printed in the United States of America
First Edition: March 2026

Dedicated to the vision of a more coherent future
for all sentient beings

Acknowledgment

We acknowledge all those who have come before us. Your coherence is not lost, only lost to our vision. Our coherence is made possible only by your coherence.

Hexagram 13

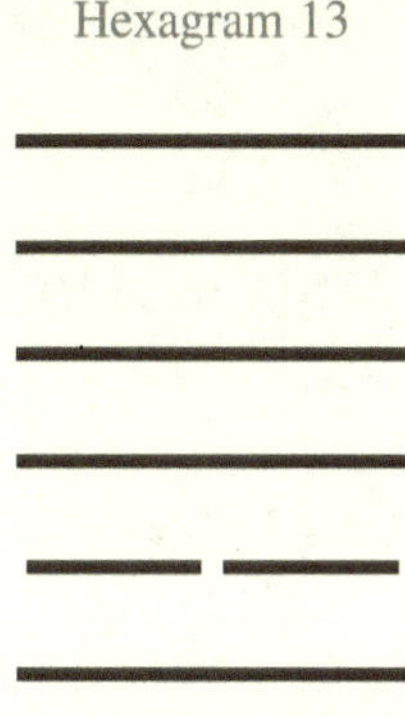

Tóng Rén — Fellowship with People

Heaven above, Fire below

Fellowship with people in the open.
Success.
It furthers one to cross the great water.
Perseverance furthers.

Fire rises toward heaven: the image of fellowship among people. True community arises not from uniformity but from the clarity that comes when diverse people organize themselves around shared principles. The warmth of fire and the vastness of heaven together suggest that genuine fellowship must be open and inclusive — not confined to faction or clan, but extended to all who share in the common work.

Such fellowship succeeds because it rests on what people hold in common rather than what divides them. It has the strength to undertake great and difficult things — to cross the great water — precisely because its foundation is broad enough to sustain the weight. The perseverance required is not rigid adherence but steady commitment to the shared vision that brought people together in the first place.

— after the Yi Jing, Wilhelm/Baynes translation

Contents

Section 1: Introduction — Why Social Dynamics Needs Coherence

Abstract

Abstract. This paper extends the Coherence Universalism (CU) framework to the domain of social dynamics. It argues that societies, institutions, economies, and cultures can be understood as coherence systems — systems whose viability depends on maintaining integrated self-regulation across multiple agents, scales, and time horizons. Part I (Sections 2–5) traces human history as a coherence trajectory, identifies the recurrent failure modes of social coherence, evaluates why prior solutions cannot scale to present conditions, and diagnoses the contemporary crisis as a historically unprecedented coherence bottleneck. Part II (Sections 7–11) develops a formal framework for social coherence dynamics: the three-field coupling model, the social coherence functional and its gradient dynamics, failure thresholds and cascade mechanisms, institutional design principles, trauma-cascade analysis, and the identification of a high-coherence social attractor. Four appendices provide a glossary, a referenced principles index, the mathematical formalization, and an application to the economics of AI-mediated production. The framework generates specific falsifiable predictions testable against cross-national datasets and identifies the structural conditions under which civilizational-scale coherence can be sustained without coercion.

1.1 The State of the Problem

Across nearly every domain of collective human life — politics, economics (see CU-EC-0 through CU-EC-11, developed in Appendix D), culture, ecology, technology — we observe a common pattern: fragmentation. Societies experience polarization, institutional breakdown, and moral incoherence. Ecological systems destabilize under pressures that no single nation or ideology can resolve. Technologies amplify agency faster than ethics can adapt. Individuals report rising anxiety, depression, and loss of meaning — not as isolated clinical events but as symptoms of a shared condition they can sense but rarely name.

These crises are typically treated as separate. Mental health is a clinical issue. Politics is an ideological conflict. Climate change is a technical problem. Culture is a matter of values. This fragmentation of explanation mirrors the fragmentation of experience itself. What is missing is a framework capable of explaining why these failures co-occur, why progress in one domain so often coincides with regression in another, and why well-intentioned interventions so reliably produce unintended consequences at other scales.

The social sciences have generated sophisticated accounts of each domain in isolation. Political science models institutional dynamics. Economics models incentive structures. Sociology models stratification and collective behavior. Anthropology maps cultural variation. Yet none of these disciplines possesses a shared foundational concept that explains why societies hold together in the first place, why they fall apart in characteristic patterns, or what structural conditions must be satisfied for collective human life to remain viable across scales and across time.

This is not a failure of effort or intelligence. It is a consequence of disciplinary fragmentation that mirrors the very phenomenon it needs to explain. The social sciences lack a concept of *social coherence* — the structural condition that determines whether collective human systems function, fragment, or collapse — and they lack it for the same reason societies are struggling: the integrative frameworks that once held these questions together have weakened faster than new ones have emerged.

1.2 The Preceding Framework

This paper is part of the Coherence Universalism (CU) series published by the Heaven≡Earth Press. It presupposes — and extends — the formal framework established in the preceding papers.

CU — M&E: The Transcendental Framework presents the Coherence Ladder, a sequence of structural rungs tracing the emergence of physical order, life, consciousness, meaning, social coordination, normativity, and governance from pure relational possibility. That paper establishes the foundational principles (CU-FP1 through CU-FP8) governing coherence at every scale: that coherence is a transcendental condition (CU-FP1), that it admits of degree and direction (CU-FP2), that constraint is essential to its realization (CU-FP3), that it operates across multiple scales simultaneously (CU-FP4), and that identity is constraint-preserved coherence (CU-FP8). It also establishes the cultural coherence principles (CU-CL-0 through CU-CL-11) that govern how civilizations generate, transmit, and destroy coherence at the collective level.

CU — Consciousness develops the forcing conditions (CF-1 through CF-5) under which coherence acquires an interior. It introduces the coherence functional C(u) on state space H, the viability region V, the distortion measure D(u), the identity conditions (CU-I1 through CU-I5), and the dynamics principles (CU-D1 through CU-D10) that govern how systems navigate coherence landscapes.

CU — Psychology extends the framework to individual psychological coherence. It introduces meaning space M (CU-Ψ1), meaning maps Φ (CU-Ψ2), the Field Coherence Score FCS (CU-Ψ3), Inverse Entropic Stress IES (CU-Ψ4), coherence drive (CU-Ψ5), local—global tension (CU-Ψ6), and shared coherence fields (CU-Ψ12). It demonstrates that every canonical domain of psychology — perception, cognition, emotion, identity, attachment, pathology, therapy — can be understood as a mechanism that either supports or undermines the maintenance of integrated self-regulation across time.

This paper picks up where psychology leaves off. The Psychology paper asks: how do individual psychological systems maintain, lose, and restore coherence? This paper asks: what happens when coherence must be maintained not within a single system but across many — and what structural conditions determine whether collective coherence holds, fragments, or collapses?

The Psychology paper established that individual coherence depends partly on the shared coherence fields (CU-Ψ12) in which the individual is embedded. It showed that therapy alone is insufficient when cultural coherence is degraded (Psychology, Appendix H), that ideology functions as compensatory coherence in fragmented social fields (Psychology, §9.3), and that the modern mental health crisis is better understood as a collective coherence crisis than as an epidemic of individual pathology (Psychology, §11.4). Each of these findings points beyond the individual — toward the social dynamics this paper develops.

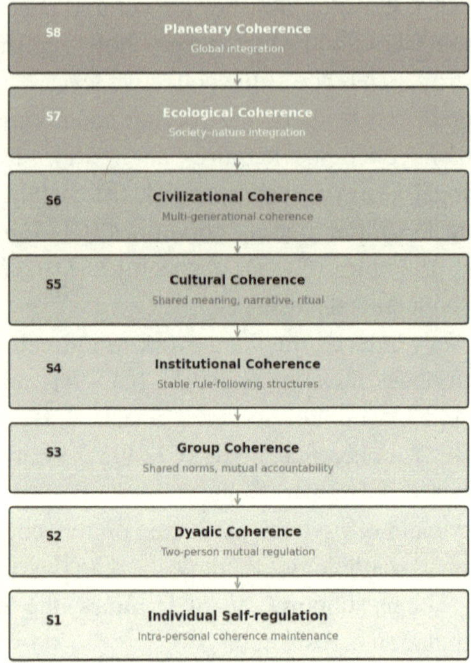

Figure 1. *The Coherence Ladder in social context. Social dynamics occupies the upper rungs, from individual self-regulation through dyadic, group, institutional, cultural, civilizational, ecological, and planetary coherence. Each rung enables and constrains those above it. The framework treats social coherence not as a metaphor but as a structural property of multi-agent systems.*

1.3 Position on the Coherence Ladder

The Coherence Ladder organizes the CU series by identifying which structural transitions each paper addresses. This paper occupies **Rungs 22 through 30** — the span from shared representations to norm justification — with particular focus on the social coherence rungs (22–26) where collective meaning, coordination, institutions, and culture emerge, and the normative coherence rungs (27–30) where ethical reasoning becomes structurally unavoidable.

— **Rung 22** (Shared Representations) is where coherence ceases to be confined to individual agents. Language, symbols, and shared practices distribute coherence across multiple systems, enabling coordination that no single agent could achieve alone. This rung marks the beginning of properly social dynamics.

— **Rung 23** (Coordination Dynamics) describes how agents adjust behavior to maintain shared coherence. Social order arises from mutual prediction, feedback, and alignment — not from external imposition. The success or failure of coordination at this rung determines whether shared representations stabilize or fragment.

— **Rung 24** (Norm Formation) captures the stabilization of coordination patterns into expectations. Norms function as attractors in social coherence space, guiding behavior without constant negotiation and reducing the cognitive load of collective life.

— **Rung 25** (Institutions) describes the formalization of norms into structures that persist beyond individual lifespans. Institutions encode constraints that stabilize social coherence across time and scale, but they also introduce rigidity — the tradeoff between stability and adaptability that characterizes every institutional form.

— **Rung 26** (Culture) is the highest-level social coherence structure. Culture integrates norms, institutions, shared representations, and practices into patterns that persist across generations. It is the memory of social systems — and, as this paper argues, the primary infrastructure through which coherence is generated, transmitted, and lost at civilizational scale.

— **Rungs 27–30** (Value Differentiation, Harm Detection, Tradeoff Resolution, Norm Justification) introduce the normative dimension of social coherence: the point at which not all stable coherence patterns are recognized as desirable, and ethical reasoning becomes structurally necessary. These rungs mark the transition from this paper's concerns to those of *CU — Ethics*, but the social conditions under which normative coherence emerges or collapses are developed here.

However, the paper's historical scope reaches back much further. To explain how contemporary societies arrived at their current coherence profile, we must trace the trajectory from pre-symbolic embodied coherence (Rungs 11–15), through the emergence of meaning and agency (Rungs 16–21), to the construction and eventual degradation of the social coherence infrastructure (Rungs 22–26) that now shows signs of systemic failure. The historical narrative in Part I of this paper is, in effect, a Ladder ascent — with characteristic failure modes at each transition.

1.4 The Central Claim

This paper advances the following thesis: human history is a sequence of coherence strategies — ways of generating, stabilizing, and transmitting coherence across individuals and societies — and the present global crisis reflects a structural mismatch between inherited coherence technologies and the scale and complexity of the world those technologies helped create.

This claim connects directly to the formal apparatus of Coherence Universalism:

— The foundational principle CU-FP4 (multi-scale coherence) requires that local coherence be compatible with global coherence. The central diagnostic of this paper is that modern societies systematically violate this requirement — achieving extraordinary coherence within domains while producing incoherence across them.

— The dynamics principle CU-D6 (multi-timescale coherence) explains why faster dynamics constrained by slower integrative structures can remain stable, while faster dynamics that outpace their integrative structures cannot. Modern technology accelerates social dynamics beyond the pace at which cultural coherence structures can adapt.

— The psychological principle CU-Ψ6 (local—global tension), established as the single most important structural principle in CU psychology, operates identically at the social scale. The locally rational strategy that produces globally irrational outcomes is not merely a psychological phenomenon — it is the defining pattern of civilizational fragmentation.

— The cultural coherence principles CU-CL-0 through CU-CL-11 specify the conditions under which cultures generate or consume coherence, shape or distort desire, renew or exhaust meaning, and permit or suppress legitimate refusal. These principles provide the normative constraints against which historical and contemporary social systems can be evaluated.

This paper extends the formal framework by introducing concepts specific to social-scale coherence dynamics, including multi-field coupling (how individual, cultural, and ecological coherence interact), meso-scale coherence structures (families, communities, organizations, movements), the Cultural Coherence Tensor (a diagnostic tool for characterizing how societies distribute coherence regulation), and social-scale failure thresholds derived from the viability conditions (CU-I5, CU-V1) applied at collective scales.

1.5 The Modern Crisis as a Coherence Crisis

The present moment is not merely one of rapid change. It is a structural convergence in which multiple coherence failures are occurring simultaneously across all major scales — individual, social, cultural, ecological, and technological — without any dominant integrative framework capable of coordinating response.

At the individual scale, the Psychology paper documented rising rates of depression, anxiety, substance use disorders, loneliness, and suicidality across developed nations (Psychology, §11.4). These are not isolated clinical events but the individual-level registration of degraded collective coherence — the felt consequence of inhabiting social fields that no longer provide the regulatory support human psychological architecture requires.

At the institutional scale, trust in governments, media, religious organizations, and civic institutions has declined steadily across developed nations over the past half-century (Putnam, 2000; Twenge et al., 2014). Institutions are the formalized coherence structures of Rung 25; their erosion removes the stabilizing constraints that made large-scale coordination possible.

At the cultural scale, the shared meaning fields that once aligned individual motivation with collective action — religious cosmologies, national narratives, ethical traditions — have weakened without being replaced by functionally equivalent structures (CU-CL-8: meaning must be renewable). The result is not liberation but meaning fragmentation: individuals constructing identity from incompatible sources, with scientific worldviews providing no moral guidance, moral intuitions lacking metaphysical grounding, and political identities operating without shared reality models.

At the ecological scale, planetary boundaries are being crossed in ways that constrain the long-term viability of every other coherence level. Ecological coherence operates on slow timescales with high inertia (CU-D6); its degradation propagates downward into cultural and individual coherence with a lag that makes the causal connection difficult to perceive but no less real.

At the technological scale, artificial intelligence, social media, and algorithmic optimization amplify existing coherence gradients without integrating them. They reward local optimization, amplify emotional salience, and bypass traditional regulatory structures — precisely the conditions under which CU-Ψ6 (local—global tension) produces maximal damage.

This paper argues that these phenomena are not five separate crises but expressions of a single underlying condition: a breakdown in coherence across scales. Understanding this condition requires both a historical perspective — how did we arrive here? — and a formal one — what structural dynamics produce these patterns and what would it take to change them?

1.6 What This Paper Does Not Claim

This paper does not argue that humanity has "lost" coherence in some absolute sense. Modern societies are capable of extraordinary local coherence: highly specialized expertise, sophisticated technologies, and powerful symbolic systems. The problem is not an absence of coherence but its uneven distribution and poor regulation across scales. The gains in domain-specific coherence have come at the cost of integration — between mind and body, individual and community, culture and ecology, short-term optimization and long-term viability.

Nor does this paper claim that any past era was a golden age of coherence. Every historical coherence strategy involved tradeoffs, exclusions, and characteristic failure modes. The task is not to return to pre-modern forms but to understand the structural dynamics that made them work within their scale — and to develop integrative coherence strategies appropriate to a planetary civilization operating under conditions no prior human society has faced.

Finally, this paper does not propose a political program, an ideology, or a moral crusade. It proposes that coherence itself — the structural condition that determines whether systems integrate or fragment — can be understood, formally characterized, and deliberately cultivated across scales, without requiring uniform belief, centralized control, or the suppression of legitimate diversity.

1.7 Structure of the Paper

The paper proceeds in two parts.

Part I: Human History as a Coherence Trajectory (Sections 2–5) tells the story of how coherence has been generated, transformed, and lost across evolutionary, cultural, and historical time. Each epoch is positioned on the Coherence Ladder, and each transition is analyzed through the CU dynamics principles that govern it.

— **Section 2** defines social coherence and introduces the formal constructs specific to this paper.

— **Section 3** traces the emergence of coherence from pre-symbolic embodied practices through symbolic systems to abstract ethical frameworks — the Ladder ascent from Rungs 11–15 through Rungs 22–26.

— Section 4 identifies the recurrent failure modes of coherence across history: embodiment loss, structural collapse, fragmented optimization, and ideological substitution, analyzed through CU-FP3, CU-Ψ6, and CU-Ψ11. It also introduces the mechanism by which individual trauma constrains collective viability space — a theme developed fully in Section 10.

— **Section 5** evaluates why prior coherence solutions — mythic-religious systems, Enlightenment rationalism, liberal individualism, nationalism, postmodern deconstruction — cannot scale forward to present conditions.

— **Section 6** presents the contemporary crisis as a coherence bottleneck: a historically unprecedented convergence of multi-scale coherence failures.

Part II: Toward Social Coherence Theory (Sections 7–11) develops the formal framework for understanding and intervening in social-scale coherence dynamics.

— Section 7 introduces multi-scale coherence dynamics: the formal analysis of how individual, cultural, and ecological coherence fields interact, building on CU-D1 and CU-FP4. It also introduces the social coherence functional — a composite measure of trust, information integrity, coordination capacity, resilience, and extraction — and its associated gradient dynamics.

— **Section 8** develops meso-scale coherence: the intermediate structures — families, communities, organizations, movements — through which most coherence dynamics actually operate.

— Section 9 formalizes failure thresholds and cascade dynamics: the conditions under which coherence collapse at one scale propagates across scales. It also identifies competing attractor basins — coherent, coercive, fragmented, extractive, and propagandist regimes — with measurable drift signatures that function as early-warning indicators.

— **Section 10** derives intervention principles: what structural conditions must be satisfied for coherence restoration at each scale, with particular attention to institutional design, community reconstruction, technology regulation, and cultural renewal.

— Section 11 develops the trauma-cascade analysis: how individual psychological injury propagates through group dynamics, institutional lock-in, economic precarity, and polarization into civilizational-scale coherence degradation — and identifies the intervention logic required to break the loop.

Section 12 identifies the social coherence attractor — a high-coherence basin whose formal properties correspond to what diverse civilizations have independently described as the ideal of just, truthful, and cooperative social organization. It also traces the connections forward to CU — Artificial Intelligence and CU — Ethics, and addresses what has and has not been established.

Appendix D applies the framework to the economics of AI-mediated production, analyzing collective cognition as a factor of production and deriving institutional design principles for coherence-stabilizing economic policy. Future appendices will develop the Cultural Coherence Tensor (a diagnostic tool for comparative cultural analysis), historical case studies, and the measurement framework for operationalizing social-scale coherence constructs.

1.8 What Would Prove This Framework Wrong

The social coherence framework advanced in this paper generates empirical commitments that are, in principle, falsifiable. Four conditions would constitute evidence against its core claims.

First, if cross-national data reveal no persistent clustering in the five-dimensional state space defined by the social coherence functional (§7.8), the attractor hypothesis fails. The framework predicts that societies cluster into recognizable regime types — not that they occupy the space uniformly.

Second, if trajectories through the state space show no directional drift toward basin centers, the gradient dynamics on which the framework relies are unsupported. Societies should not move randomly through coherence space; they should be drawn toward or repelled from identifiable attractors.

Third, if no early-warning signatures — rising variance, increasing autocorrelation in coherence indicators — precede known collapse events, the cascade dynamics central to the paper's analytical apparatus lack empirical support.

Fourth, if recovery paths are symmetric with collapse paths, the hysteresis predictions that distinguish genuine attractor dynamics from simple fluctuation are disconfirmed.

Section 9.9 develops the operationalization framework for these tests. Section 12.7 addresses the broader epistemic limits of what has and has not been established. The framework is offered as a testable proposal, not a finished theory.

Section 2: What Social Coherence Is

The Psychology paper established that individual coherence is a system-level achievement — the integrated, constraint-satisfying organization of perception, emotion, cognition, identity, and action across time. It also established, particularly in Section 10, that individual coherence is not self-contained. Human psychological architecture evolved for distributed regulation: the individual mind achieves and maintains coherence partly through structures that extend beyond it — shared representations, coordinated expectations, stabilized norms, formalized institutions, and the cultural memory that transmits coherence strategies across generations.

This paper takes up the question that finding implies. If individual coherence depends on collective structures, then those collective structures themselves must be understood as coherence systems — systems that can be more or less coherent, that can maintain or lose viability, that navigate their own coherence landscapes, and that are subject to their own characteristic failure modes. Social coherence is not merely the sum of individual coherences. It is a structural property of the collective that emerges from, constrains, and partially constitutes the coherence of its members.

This section defines social coherence formally and introduces the concepts specific to this paper.

2.1 Social Coherence as Distributed Regulatory Integration

A society is not a single agent. It is a system of systems — an ensemble of agents, relationships, practices, norms, institutions, narratives, and material infrastructure that must coordinate across space, time, and scale to remain viable. Social coherence refers to the degree to which these components mutually support one another rather than interfere, fragment, or work at cross-purposes.

This definition extends CU-FP1 (Coherence as Transcendental Condition) to the social domain — instantiating CU-S1 (The Distributed Coherence Principle): social coherence is coherence distributed across multiple agents via shared representations. Just as coherence is the condition of possibility for a functioning mind, social coherence is the condition of possibility for a functioning society. A population of individuals who cannot coordinate — who share no representations, follow no norms, sustain no institutions, and transmit no cultural memory — does not constitute a society in any meaningful sense. It constitutes an aggregate.

The formal apparatus of the preceding papers applies at the social scale with appropriate modifications. A social system occupies a configuration in a state space whose dimensions include the distributions of individual coherence states, the structure and content of shared representations, the stability and legitimacy of norms and institutions, the health of material and ecological infrastructure, and the temporal depth of cultural memory. Social coherence is measurable, in principle, as the degree of integrated mutual constraint across these components — the degree to which changes in one component are absorbed and regulated rather than amplified into cascading disruption.

The viability region V, defined for individual systems by the identity conditions CU-I1 through CU-I5, has a social analog. A society remains viable when its configuration satisfies the constraints necessary for continued coordinated functioning. These constraints include: the capacity to maintain shared representations under disagreement (Rung 22), the capacity to coordinate behavior through mutual adjustment (Rung 23), the stability of normative expectations (Rung 24), the functional legitimacy of institutions (Rung 25; CU-S5, CU-E-10), and the integrative capacity of cultural frameworks (Rung 26). When too many of these constraints are violated simultaneously, the society exits its viability region — not in the dramatic sense of physical destruction, but in the structural sense of losing the capacity for coordinated response to challenges. The society may persist as a geographic entity while ceasing to function as a coherence system.

2.2 Social Coherence Is Not Consensus

A crucial clarification must be made immediately, because its absence has distorted social theory for centuries.

Social coherence is not agreement. It is not uniformity. It is not consensus. It is not the suppression of dissent or the elimination of conflict.

Two people may disagree profoundly and still participate in a coherent social system — provided their disagreement occurs within a framework of shared representations, mutual intelligibility, and institutional structures capable of managing conflict without collapse. Two people may agree completely and still generate social incoherence — if their agreement produces a local alignment that degrades coordination at larger scales (CU-Ψ6).

This follows directly from CU-FP3 (Constraint Is Essential to Coherence). Coherence requires constraint, but not any particular constraint. What matters is that the constraints are mutually compatible across scales and sufficient to maintain viability — not that everyone agrees on their content. A courtroom in which opposing lawyers argue vigorously is more socially coherent than a boardroom in which everyone agrees to a plan that will bankrupt the company. The courtroom has procedural coherence: shared rules, mutual intelligibility, institutional structure, and mechanisms for resolution. The boardroom has consensus without integration — agreement that masks an absence of critical examination.

This distinction explains why societies that prize ideological uniformity are often less resilient than societies that tolerate structured disagreement. Uniformity achieves local coherence (within the ideology) at the cost of global coherence (the system's capacity to detect and correct error). CU-CL-11 (Narratives Must Permit Refusal) makes this a formal requirement: cultural narratives that cannot accommodate dissent without rendering dissenters unintelligible have eliminated a necessary constraint on their own coherence — the constraint of reality-testing that only genuine disagreement can provide.

2.3 The Three Coherence Fields

The preceding papers operate primarily at the individual scale, with social and ecological dimensions referenced but not formalized. This paper introduces a multi-field framework that makes the coupling between scales explicit.

We define three coherence fields, each representing a domain with its own characteristic dynamics, timescales, and viability conditions:

The individual field **(C_i)** encompasses psychological, embodied, and identity-level coherence as developed in *CU — Psychology*. Its dynamics are governed by the CU-Ψ principles, its timescales range from milliseconds (perception) to decades (identity development), and its viability is defined by the individual's capacity to maintain integrated self-regulation. C_i is what the Psychology paper analyzed.

The cultural field **(C_c)** encompasses the coherence of shared representations, norms, institutions, and cultural memory — the structures corresponding to Ladder Rungs 22 through 26. Its dynamics are governed by the CU-CL principles, its timescales range from years (norm formation) to centuries (cultural transmission), and its viability is defined by the society's capacity to coordinate action, manage conflict, transmit meaning, and adapt to changing conditions. C_c is this paper's primary subject.

The ecological field **(C_e)** encompasses the coherence of environmental, material, and planetary systems that constrain the viability of both individuals and cultures. Its dynamics operate on timescales from decades (resource cycles) to millennia (climate systems), and its viability is defined by the biosphere's capacity to sustain the material conditions for life. C_e enters this paper as a boundary condition and coupling term rather than a primary subject — its full development awaits a future paper — but its inclusion is essential because ecological constraints are among the most powerful determinants of social coherence trajectories.

The central formal claim of this paper is that these fields are coupled: each field's dynamics depend on the states of the others, and coherence failure at one scale propagates across scales in characteristic patterns. The coupling is bidirectional but asymmetric — a feature whose implications will be developed throughout the paper (Section 7).

This multi-field framework is an application of CU-FP4 (Multi-Scale Coherence) and CU-D6 (Multi-Timescale Coherence) at the social scale. CU-FP4 requires that local coherence be compatible with global coherence; the multi-field framework specifies what "global" means when multiple coherence systems with different timescales and dynamics are interacting. CU-D6 requires that faster dynamics be constrained by slower integrative structures; the multi-field framework specifies the mechanisms through which that constraint operates — and the consequences when it fails.

2.4 Coherence Infrastructure and Coherence Channeling

Culture generates coherence, but it does not do so in a vacuum. Coherence generation depends on infrastructure — the material, institutional, and symbolic substrate through which coherence is produced, maintained, and transmitted. CU-CL-0 identifies culture as the coherence infrastructure of civilization. This paper develops that identification into an analytic framework.

Coherence infrastructure refers to the ensemble of structures — both material and symbolic — through which a society generates and maintains coherence across its members. This includes: physical infrastructure (transportation, communication, energy systems) that enables coordination across distance; institutional infrastructure (legal systems, educational systems, governance structures) that stabilizes norms and manages conflict across time; symbolic infrastructure (shared language, narrative traditions, artistic forms, ritual practices) that generates and transmits meaning; and relational infrastructure (families, communities, voluntary associations) that provides the distributed regulation on which individual coherence depends.

Infrastructure is not coherence itself, but the substrate without which coherence cannot be generated at scale. A city may have excellent infrastructure and poor coherence (if its institutions have lost legitimacy) or poor infrastructure and remarkable coherence (if its communities have strong relational bonds that compensate). But infrastructure places an upper bound on the coherence a society can sustain under pressure. Under normal conditions, coherence can exceed what infrastructure alone would predict; under stress, coherence contracts toward what infrastructure can support.

Coherence channeling refers to the way social structures shape not just the magnitude but the direction of coherence flow. Cultures do not merely enable or inhibit coherence; they direct it toward particular configurations and away from others. A society that channels coherence primarily through market mechanisms will produce one pattern of integration (high economic coordination, weak communal bonds). A society that channels coherence primarily through kinship will produce a different pattern (strong family cohesion, limited institutional trust beyond kin networks). A society that channels coherence primarily through ideological conformity will produce yet another (high symbolic alignment, brittle response to internal dissent).

Coherence channeling explains why societies with similar levels of aggregate coherence can exhibit radically different profiles of strength and vulnerability. The total coherence may be comparable, but its distribution across domains — material, relational, symbolic, institutional — determines which stresses the society can absorb and which will produce cascade failure. The Cultural Coherence Tensor developed in Appendix A provides a formal diagnostic tool for characterizing these distributions.

2.5 Meso-Scale Coherence

One of the most significant gaps in both social theory and the current CU framework is the treatment of intermediate structures — the social formations that are larger than individuals but smaller than civilizations. Families, friendships, neighborhoods, congregations, workplaces, professional communities, civic organizations, local governments, social movements, and online communities all function as coherence intermediaries: they receive regulatory support from the cultural field above them, provide regulatory support to the individuals embedded within them, and generate coherence dynamics of their own that are reducible to neither level.

These meso-scale structures are where most social coherence is actually generated and maintained in daily life. The grand cultural narratives, institutional frameworks, and civilizational meaning systems that this paper analyzes at the macro scale are experienced by individuals primarily through meso-scale mediation. A person's relationship to their nation's political institutions is mediated by their community's engagement with those institutions. A person's access to cultural meaning is mediated by the specific practices, relationships, and organizations through which that meaning is transmitted.

The meso-scale is also where coherence is most amenable to deliberate intervention. Civilizational dynamics operate on timescales too long for individual agency to affect directly. Individual psychology operates on timescales too fast for institutional design to regulate precisely. Meso-scale structures occupy the temporal middle ground — they can be built, reformed, or restored within the span of a human life, and they mediate between the civilizational coherence infrastructure that individuals cannot change alone and the individual coherence needs that civilizations cannot address directly.

The erosion of meso-scale structures is, as Putnam (2000) documented extensively, one of the defining features of late modernity.

The decline of civic organizations, religious congregations, community associations, extended family networks, and local institutions removes the primary mechanism through which individuals access distributed coherence regulation. This produces a characteristic modern pattern: individuals are connected to the cultural field through increasingly thin, one-directional channels — mass media, social media, consumer culture — that transmit information without providing regulation, and that extract attention without generating belonging. The result is high informational exposure with low relational support: precisely the conditions under which individual IES (CU-Ψ4) escalates while the distributed regulatory capacity that could absorb it diminishes.

Section 8 develops the analysis of meso-scale coherence in detail.

2.6 What This Paper Introduces

To summarize the conceptual apparatus specific to this paper:

Multi-field coupling. The formal treatment of how individual (C_i), cultural (C_c), and ecological (C_e) coherence interact — including the coupling mechanisms, the characteristic timescales, the asymmetries of influence, and the cascade dynamics through which failure propagates across scales. This is the paper's primary formal contribution, developed in Section 6.

Social-scale viability. The application of the identity conditions (CU-I1 through CU-I5) and viability conditions (CU-V1 through CU-V7) to social systems, defining the structural thresholds beyond which coordinated social functioning breaks down. Developed in Section 8.

Coherence infrastructure. The material, institutional, symbolic, and relational substrate through which societies generate and maintain coherence. Extends CU-CL-0 into an analytic framework. Applied throughout.

Coherence channeling. The directional shaping of coherence flow by social structures — how cultures determine not just the level but the pattern of coherence their members can achieve. Applied throughout; formally characterized through the Cultural Coherence Tensor (Appendix A).

Meso-scale coherence. The analysis of intermediate social structures (families through movements) as coherence intermediaries that mediate between individual and civilizational scales. Developed in Section 7.

The Cultural Coherence Tensor. A diagnostic tool for characterizing how societies distribute coherence regulation across structural, symbolic, embodied, and meaning-generating domains, enabling systematic comparison of coherence strategies across cultures and historical periods. Developed in Appendix A.

These concepts do not replace the existing CU apparatus. They extend it to the social scale — providing the vocabulary needed to analyze coherence dynamics at the level where most of human history, most of human suffering, and most of the available leverage for change actually operate.

Cultural Coherence Tensor. These constructs extend the CU framework to the domain where coordination (CU-S2) and institutional maintenance (CU-S3) determine collective viability.

This section has defined social coherence as distributed regulatory integration across multiple agents, scales, and time horizons — not consensus or agreement but the structural capacity of a collective to maintain viability under constraint. The three-field model (individual C_i, cultural C_c, ecological C_e), the Social Coherence Tensor, and the Coherence Infrastructure concept provide the formal tools for the analysis that follows.

Section 3: Human History as a Coherence Trajectory

Human history can be understood as a sequence of increasingly ambitious attempts to generate, stabilize, and transmit coherence across growing numbers of agents, expanding geographical scales, and lengthening time horizons. Each major epoch corresponds to a structural transition on the Coherence Ladder — the construction of a new rung of social coherence — and each transition brings both expanded capacity and new vulnerability.

This section traces that trajectory from pre-symbolic embodied coherence through the emergence of symbolic systems, the Axial revolution, and the modern amplification of local coherence at global cost. It is not a comprehensive history but a structural narrative: the story of how the Ladder was climbed, and why the climbing itself produces the characteristic tradeoffs that define the present crisis.

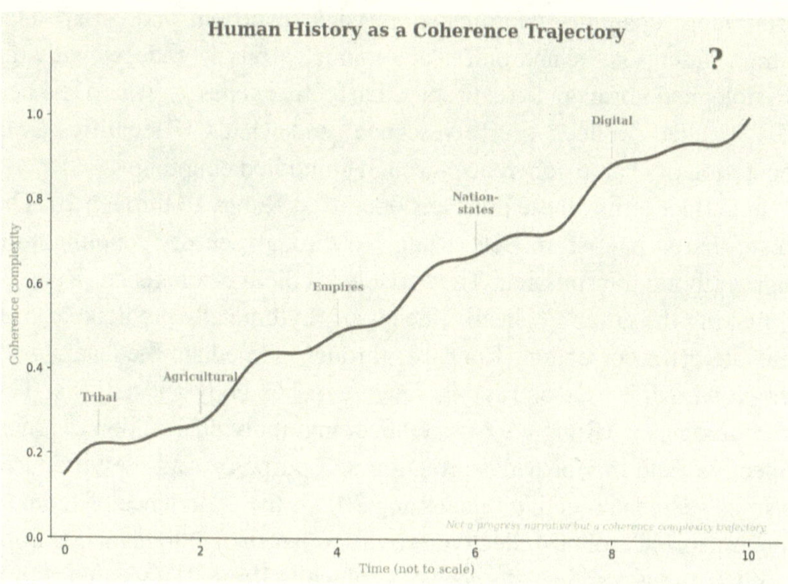

Figure 2. Human history as a coherence trajectory. From embodied pre-symbolic coordination through the symbolic revolution, institutional development, the Axial age, and modern fragmentation to the present crisis. The dashed line indicates the hypothesized path toward a high-coherence attractor. The trajectory is non-monotonic: modernity amplified capacity but fragmented integration.

3.1 Embodied Coherence: Before Symbols (Rungs 11–20)

Long before coherence became a philosophical concern or a mathematical variable, it was a matter of survival. Early human groups faced environments characterized by uncertainty, scarcity, predation, and rapid change. The capacity to coordinate perception, action, emotion, and intention across individuals was not optional — it was the primary selective advantage that allowed anatomically modern humans to outcompete larger, stronger, or faster species (Tomasello, 2014; Henrich, 2016).

Crucially, this coordination was not primarily conceptual. It was embodied and enacted.

Archaeological and anthropological evidence suggests that early human coherence emerged through practices rather than beliefs. Rhythmic movement, synchronized labor, vocalization, and shared ritual activity appear across virtually all known early cultures (McNeill, 1995). These practices achieve something that no purely cognitive mechanism can: they align nervous systems across multiple agents simultaneously. Drumming, chanting, coordinated physical exertion, and group dance entrain attention, synchronize autonomic arousal, reduce individual physiological noise, and create shared affective states — what Durkheim (1912) called "collective effervescence" and what CU identifies as the generation of shared coherence through embodied coupling.

In Ladder terms, these practices operate at Rungs 16 through 20. They create shared internal models (Rung 16) through sensory coupling rather than symbolic transmission. They enable predictive coherence (Rung 17) by making the group's collective behavior rhythmically predictable. They generate error correction (Rung 18) through immediate feedback — the person who falls out of rhythm feels it in her body and adjusts. They support agency (Rung 19) by embedding individual action within a collective field that provides direction and purpose. And they produce a form of shared subjective time (Rung 20) — the experience of temporal flow organized around collective activity rather than individual cognition.

What these practices do not yet achieve is Rung 21 (Meaning) in its full symbolic sense, or any of the social rungs (22–26). Meaning exists, but it is lived rather than represented — a felt sense of belonging, purpose, and orientation within the group that does not depend on, and may not even be expressible in, propositional form. Coherence is real but implicit: generated through practice, maintained through repetition, and transmitted through participation rather than instruction.

This form of coherence has a crucial limitation: it is scale-sensitive. Embodied synchrony operates most effectively at group sizes below Dunbar's (1992) number — approximately 150 individuals, the maximum group size that can be maintained through direct personal relationships. Beyond this threshold, the regulatory mechanisms of embodied coherence begin to fail. You cannot synchronize nervous systems across a population of thousands through drumming alone. The practices that generate coherence at the band or village scale do not generalize to the city, the kingdom, or the civilization.

But within its proper scale, embodied coherence is remarkably robust. Communities organized around shared practice, direct reciprocity, and ritualized coordination have persisted for tens of thousands of years. The fragility belongs not to the mechanism but to its scale constraints — a fragility that becomes consequential only when populations grow beyond the mechanism's reach.

3.2 The Symbolic Revolution: Storing and Transmitting Coherence (Rungs 21–22)

As populations grew and social structures became more complex, embodied coherence alone could no longer sustain coordination. Larger groups required mechanisms to stabilize meaning across distance, time, and kinship boundaries. This pressure produced the most consequential innovation in the history of social coherence: symbolic representation.

The emergence of language, and with it myth, narrative, and early moral norms, corresponds to the Ladder's transition to Rung 21 (Meaning) in its full sense and Rung 22 (Shared Representations). Where embodied coherence generates integration through felt participation, symbolic coherence generates integration through shared content — stories, rules, categories, and explanations that multiple agents can represent, recall, and transmit independently of direct bodily co-presence.

Symbols allowed coherence to be stored and transmitted in ways that embodied practices could not. Stories encoded social rules, preserving solutions to coordination problems across generations. Myths situated individuals within cosmic order, providing identity-level coherence (who we are, where we come from, what the world means) that extended beyond the immediate perceptual horizon. Ritual linked embodied practices to symbolic meaning, anchoring abstract content in lived experience — a coupling between the pre-symbolic and symbolic coherence layers that proved essential to the stability of both.

This last point deserves emphasis. The emergence of symbolic coherence did not replace embodied coherence. In every known early culture, symbolic systems were layered on top of embodied practices and functioned in tight integration with them. Myths were not merely believed; they were enacted in ritual. Moral norms were not merely stated; they were embodied in daily practice. Cosmological beliefs were not merely intellectual commitments; they were lived orientations maintained through participation in collective life. There was little distinction between psychology, cosmology, and ethics — all were aspects of what Section 2.4 calls a single coherence ecology.

This integration — between embodied and symbolic coherence, between bottom-up regulation and top-down meaning — was itself a coherence achievement. And, as Section 4 will show, its dissolution is one of the most common and consequential failure modes in the history of civilization.

The symbolic revolution also introduced a new coherence mechanism: cultural transmission (Henrich, 2016). Where genetic evolution transmits coherence strategies across generations through biological reproduction (a slow process limited by generation time), cultural transmission does so through learning, imitation, and instruction — a process that can accumulate innovations indefinitely and transmit them rapidly. CU-D7 (The Novelty Principle) operates here at the population level: cultural evolution navigates coherence landscapes far more efficiently than genetic evolution alone, because it can store, combine, and recombine solutions to coordination problems without waiting for genetic recombination.

The result was an extraordinary acceleration in the complexity of social coherence. Within a few thousand years of the emergence of fully symbolic language, human societies developed agriculture, permanent settlement, social stratification, specialized labor, legal codes, writing systems, and the first large-scale institutions. Each of these developments represents a new mechanism for generating, storing, or transmitting coherence across scales that embodied practices alone could never have reached.

3.3 Coordination, Norms, and Institutions: Building the Social Rungs (Rungs 23–25)

The Ladder's social rungs — Coordination Dynamics (23), Norm Formation (24), and Institutions (25) — were not constructed in a single moment. They emerged through a long process of trial, failure, and consolidation that spans the Neolithic revolution, the emergence of the first states, and the development of the legal, religious, and administrative structures that made large-scale societies possible.

Coordination dynamics (Rung 23) describe how agents adjust behavior to maintain shared coherence through mutual prediction, feedback, and alignment — the mechanism formalized as CU-S2 (The Coordination Principle). In small groups, coordination operates through direct interaction — you can see what others are doing and adjust accordingly. As groups expand beyond the range of direct observation, coordination requires increasingly sophisticated mechanisms: division of labor, role specialization, status hierarchies, and eventually formal command structures. Each mechanism extends the range of coordinated action but also introduces new rigidity. The chieftain who coordinates a village of 200 has different flexibility than the bureaucracy that coordinates an empire of millions.

Norm formation (Rung 24) captures the stabilization of coordination patterns into expectations. When a coordination solution works repeatedly, it ceases to be a mere behavioral regularity and becomes a norm — a shared expectation that guides behavior without requiring constant negotiation. Norms function as attractors in social coherence space: they reduce the cognitive and emotional load of coordination by constraining the range of behaviors that must be anticipated and evaluated. This reduction in coordination cost is what makes complex societies possible. Without norms, every interaction would require negotiation from first principles — a load that exceeds human cognitive capacity at any scale above the small group.

But norms also constrain. A norm that solves one coordination problem may create another. Norms that stabilize gender roles may enable household coordination while suppressing individual flourishing. Norms that stabilize economic exchange may enable market coordination while externalizing ecological cost. Every norm is simultaneously a coherence generator (reducing coordination burden within its domain) and a potential coherence constraint (limiting adaptation outside its domain). This dual character — enabling and constraining — is not a flaw of norms but their structural nature. It is also why norm revision is always costly: changing a norm destabilizes the coordination it was maintaining, imposing transition costs that must be absorbed before the new norm can stabilize.

Institutions (Rung 25) emerge when norms are formalized and enforced across time and scale — instantiating CU-S3 (The Institutional Coherence Principle): institutions are mechanisms for maintaining social coherence across time and agent turnover. An institution is a norm-complex that has been given material, legal, or organizational embodiment — a court system, a religious hierarchy, a university, a market regulatory structure. Institutions solve the problem of temporal extension: they allow coherence strategies to persist beyond the individuals who developed them, beyond the circumstances that gave rise to them, and beyond the communities that first practiced them.

This temporal extension is an enormous achievement. It allows societies to accumulate coherence across generations, building on solutions developed by predecessors rather than starting fresh. But it introduces a new and characteristic failure mode: institutional drift. Because institutions persist beyond their founding conditions, they can continue to enforce norms that no longer serve the coordination problems for which they were originally designed. The institution continues to generate local coherence (internal consistency, procedural regularity, organizational stability) while its contribution to global coherence degrades — the local—global tension of CU-Ψ6 operating at the institutional scale. Section 4 treats this failure mode in detail.

3.4 Culture: The Memory of Social Systems (Rung 26)

Culture integrates norms, institutions, shared representations, and practices into relatively stable patterns that persist across generations. It is, as the Ladder specifies, the memory of social systems (CU-S4: The Cultural Transmission Principle) — the mechanism through which coherence strategies outlive the individuals who developed them and the circumstances that gave rise to them.

Cultural coherence operates at the longest timescale of any social structure. Individual coherence shifts on timescales of seconds to decades. Norms shift on timescales of years to generations. Institutions shift on timescales of decades to centuries. Culture shifts on timescales of centuries to millennia. This temporal depth provides extraordinary stability — a culture can absorb perturbations that would destroy any shorter-timescale structure — but also extraordinary inertia. When conditions change faster than cultural adaptation can respond, the resulting lag between inherited coherence strategies and present demands produces the structural mismatch that defines the modern crisis.

CU-CL-0 (Culture as Coherence Infrastructure) identifies culture as the substrate on which civilizational coherence depends. The CU-CL principles specify the conditions under which this substrate remains viable: culture must coordinate large-scale action through shared meaning (CU-CL-1), it must shape desire rather than merely constrain behavior (CU-CL-2), it must create coherence rather than merely extract it (CU-CL-3 vs. CU-CL-4), it must allow meaning to be renewed rather than merely consumed (CU-CL-8), and it must bound desire to prevent infinite escalation (CU-CL-9).

When these conditions are satisfied, culture functions as a generative coherence infrastructure — a system that produces more coherence than it consumes, enabling its members to navigate complexity that would overwhelm any individual and to transmit navigational wisdom across centuries. When these conditions are violated, culture becomes extractive — consuming the coherence of its members to maintain its own institutional stability, a dynamic that CU-CL-4 identifies as the pathological form of cultural organization.

3.5 The Axial Revolution: Abstract Coherence and Its Dangers (Rungs 27–30 Attempted)

The so-called Axial Age (roughly 800–200 BCE), identified by Jaspers (1953) and extensively analyzed by Bellah (2011) and Eisenstadt (1986), marks a profound inflection point in the history of social coherence. Across multiple civilizations — India, China, Greece, Persia, Israel — new forms of abstraction emerged: formal philosophy, universal ethics, metaphysical speculation, and reflective selfhood.

In Ladder terms, the Axial revolution represents the first sustained attempt to construct the normative rungs — Value Differentiation (27), Harm Detection (28), Tradeoff Resolution (29), and Norm Justification

(30). Pre-Axial societies had norms, but they were largely unreflective: inherited, practiced, and enforced without systematic justification. Axial thinkers asked, for the first time at civilizational scale, whether inherited norms were good — whether the coordination patterns that had stabilized social life were genuinely desirable or merely habitual.

This capacity for normative reflection dramatically expanded humanity's coherence reach. Ethical systems could now generalize beyond tribe and kin. Individuals could regulate behavior through internalized principles rather than immediate social feedback. Metaphysical frameworks offered explanations that transcended local context, enabling shared meaning across cultural and geographical boundaries. The great religions and philosophical traditions — Buddhism, Confucianism, Greek philosophy, Jewish prophetic tradition, Zoroastrianism — are all, in CU terms, attempts to construct normative coherence infrastructure capable of operating at civilizational scale.

But the Axial revolution also introduced a vulnerability that would prove consequential across the following two millennia: **the detachment of abstract coherence from embodied integration**.

When symbolic and normative systems become sufficiently abstract, they can achieve internal consistency without maintaining connection to the embodied and relational practices that originally grounded them. CU-FP3 (Constraint Is Essential to Coherence) specifies that coherence without constraint collapses into fantasy. At the Axial transition, the relevant constraint was the constraint of embodiment — the requirement that abstract principles remain connected to lived experience, bodily practice, and the concrete coordination problems of daily life. When this constraint is maintained, abstract coherence extends and enriches embodied coherence. When it is lost, abstract coherence becomes self-referential — internally consistent but disconnected from the reality it was meant to illuminate.

This is the structural origin of what the modern world calls ideology, dogma, and moralism: top-down coherence strategies that substitute symbolic consistency for lived integration. They emerge not from stupidity or malice but from the structural vulnerability inherent in any system capable of abstract representation — the same vulnerability that CU-Ψ11 (self-deception) identifies at the individual level, now operating at civilizational scale.

Different Axial civilizations navigated this tradeoff differently. Some maintained strong ritual and embodied grounding alongside their abstract developments — Hindu and Buddhist traditions retained meditation, yoga, and ritual practice as counterweights to philosophical abstraction. Others privileged doctrinal consistency and institutional authority — late-stage Roman Christianity increasingly enforced belief while weakening embodied practice. These choices produced different long-term coherence profiles, shaping the civilizational trajectories that followed for centuries.

3.6 Modernity: Fragmented Amplification

Modernity — the period from roughly the sixteenth century to the present — represents the most dramatic amplification of local coherence in human history, accompanied by the most systematic degradation of global coherence.

Scientific rationality, bureaucratic institutions, industrial production, market economies, and technological systems allow unprecedented levels of domain-specific coherence. Scientific disciplines achieve extraordinary internal consistency. Engineering systems achieve extraordinary precision. Economic systems achieve extraordinary allocative efficiency within their domains. Each represents a genuine coherence achievement — real integration, real problem-solving, real mastery of complexity within a bounded domain.

However, these gains come at a structural cost that CU-Ψ6 (local—global tension) makes precise. Each domain-specific coherence achievement optimizes within its own boundaries while externalizing costs to other domains, other timescales, and other scales of organization. Economic systems optimize efficiency while externalizing ecological cost. Political systems stabilize power while eroding interpersonal trust. Scientific disciplines achieve internal rigor while becoming mutually unintelligible. Individuals gain autonomy while losing the distributed regulation that communal structures once provided.

In CU terms, modernity maximizes local coherence while allowing the coupling between coherence fields to degrade. The individual field C_i, the cultural field C_c, and the ecological field C_e become increasingly decoupled — each following its own dynamics without the integrative constraints that previously kept them aligned. This is not a failure of intelligence or values. It is a structural consequence of coherence amplification without corresponding amplification of integrative capacity.

The Enlightenment — modernity's foundational intellectual movement — illustrates the pattern precisely. It correctly identified arbitrary authority, superstitious belief, and institutional corruption as coherence failures. Its proposed solutions — empirical reasoning, individual rights, institutional checks and balances — were genuine coherence innovations that solved real problems. But the Enlightenment also systematically weakened the integrative mechanisms it could not formalize: embodied practice, communal ritual, relational regulation, and the felt dimension of meaning. By grounding coherence exclusively in reason and empirical fact, it severed the connection between abstract understanding and embodied integration — completing at the civilizational level the detachment that the Axial age had initiated.

Weber (1905) described this as "disenchantment" — the progressive rationalization of the world that eliminates mystery, meaning, and sacred order in favor of calculability and control. In CU terms, disenchantment is the progressive weakening of Rung 26 (Culture) — specifically, the erosion of the symbolic and ritual infrastructure through which meaning, identity, and belonging were generated and transmitted. What replaces it is not meaninglessness per se but a structural condition in which meaning must be individually constructed rather than culturally provided — a demand that exceeds most individuals' regulatory capacity (as the Psychology paper documented in §11.4) and that produces the characteristic modern syndrome of high information, low integration.

3.7 The Trajectory Summarized

The history of social coherence is not a linear ascent or a simple decline. It is a tradeoff-laden trajectory in which each expansion of coherence capacity introduces new vulnerability:

Embodied coherence (Rungs 11–20) achieved profound integration within small groups but could not scale beyond Dunbar's number. Symbolic coherence (Rungs 21–22) enabled storage and transmission across distance and time but introduced the possibility of detachment from embodiment. Coordination, norms, and institutions (Rungs 23–25) enabled large-scale coordination but introduced institutional drift and the rigidity-adaptability tradeoff. Culture (Rung 26) enabled civilizational memory but introduced inertia that resists adaptation when conditions change. Axial abstraction (Rungs 27–30) enabled universal ethics and reflective normativity but introduced the vulnerability of self-referential coherence disconnected from lived constraint. Modernity amplified all of these dynamics — achieving extraordinary local coherence while degrading the coupling mechanisms that integrate across scales.

Each transition is an application of CU-D7 (The Novelty Principle): genuine innovation in coherence strategy, generating solutions to coordination problems that previous strategies could not address. And each transition produces the conditions for its own characteristic failure — not because the innovation was wrong but because every coherence strategy has a domain of validity, and extending it beyond that domain converts a solution into a problem.

The next section examines these failure modes systematically.

Section 4: Failure Modes of Social Coherence Across History

If coherence is an evolutionary achievement, then history is not a linear story of its steady accumulation. It is a punctuated record of coherence gains followed by coherence failures — cycles in which successful coordination strategies overshoot their domain of validity, rigidify under stress, and eventually collapse or are replaced by new forms. Understanding these failure modes is essential. Without them, the present moment appears chaotic or morally inexplicable. With them, modern crises become structurally legible.

The Psychology paper analyzed individual-level compensatory strategies — the ways psychological systems sacrifice long-term integration for short-term viability (Psychology, §7.4). This section identifies the social-structural analogs: the recurrent patterns through which collective coherence degrades, analyzed through the CU apparatus that makes them formally precise.

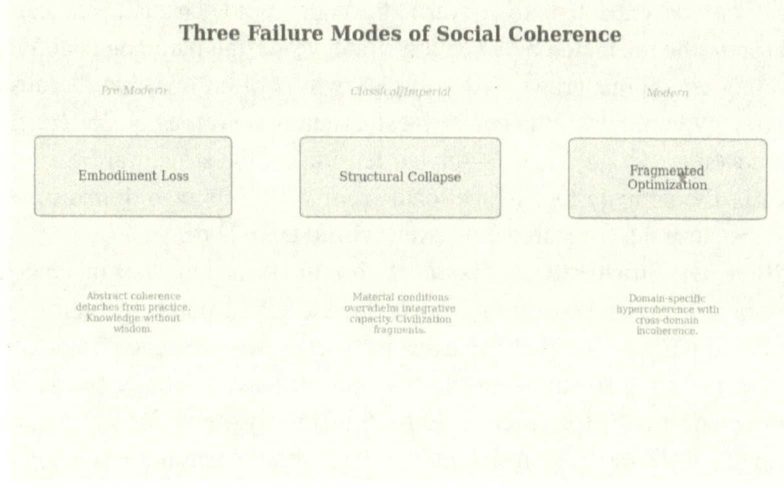

Figure 3. Historical failure modes of social coherence. Three recurring patterns: embodiment loss (abstract coherence detaches from practice), structural collapse (embodied communities cannot sustain coordination at scale), and fragmented optimization (maximizing local metrics while degrading global integration).

4.1 The General Pattern of Social Coherence Collapse

Across scales and eras, social coherence failure follows a remarkably consistent five-stage pattern. This is not a metaphor or a loose analogy; each stage corresponds to specific CU principles operating at the social scale.

Stage 1: Local optimization succeeds. A coherence strategy — ritual, institution, ideology, technology — solves a real coordination problem within a specific context. The strategy is adaptive within its original domain. It generates genuine coherence, reducing coordination costs and enabling collective action that would otherwise be impossible. This stage is governed by CU-D1 (the Universal Flow Equation): the system moves along coherence gradients toward configurations of greater integration.

Stage 2: Scale expansion outpaces integration. The strategy is extended to larger populations, faster timescales, or more abstract domains without the corresponding regulatory mechanisms that the new scale requires. A norm that stabilizes a village is imposed on a province. A coordination mechanism designed for direct interaction is applied to bureaucratic management. An institutional form that works under stable conditions is expected to govern through rapid change. At each expansion, the mismatch between the strategy's design parameters and its operating conditions grows — but the growth is often invisible, because the strategy continues to generate local coherence even as global coherence degrades. CU-Ψ6 (local—global tension) is the structural principle at work: the strategy looks functional from within its own domain precisely because the costs are being externalized elsewhere.

Stage 3: Substitution displaces integration. As the mismatch between strategy and conditions grows, the system responds by intensifying the strategy rather than revising it. Top-down coherence begins to replace rather than integrate bottom-up regulation, or vice versa. Doctrine substitutes for practice. Enforcement substitutes for legitimacy. Ideology substitutes for understanding. This is compensatory coherence at the social scale — the collective analog of the individual defense mechanisms described in Psychology §7.4. The system is not strengthening itself; it is rigidifying against the incoherence it cannot resolve.

Stage 4: Feedback degradation. The substitution of Stage 3 weakens the system's capacity to detect and respond to its own failures. Feedback loops that once connected the system to its operating conditions become attenuated: dissent is suppressed (violating CU-CL-11: narratives must permit refusal), inconvenient evidence is filtered, institutional self-assessment becomes performative rather than diagnostic. Error correction (Rung 18) — the mechanism through which systems maintain alignment with reality — degrades. The system's meaning map becomes increasingly distorted relative to the territory, in the same structural pattern that CU-Ψ11 (self-deception) describes at the individual level, now operating collectively.

Stage 5: Brittle collapse. The system appears stable — sometimes impressively so — until it encounters stress that exceeds the narrowing range its rigidified strategies can absorb. At that point, collapse is not gradual but catastrophic: the system fragments along the fault lines created by its accumulated local—global misalignments. What appears to observers as sudden breakdown was, in structural terms, long prepared by the progressive degradation of Stages 2–4.

This five-stage pattern is an application of CU-I5 (Identity Collapse Thresholds) and CU-FP7 (Coherence Collapse) at the social scale. Social systems, like individuals, have genuine collapse thresholds — critical boundaries beyond which recovery as the same system is impossible. And social systems, like individuals, often approach those thresholds gradually while appearing stable, because the compensatory mechanisms of Stages 3–4 mask the accumulating distortion.

Tainter (1988) documented this pattern across multiple civilizations: the Roman Empire, the Maya, the Western Chou dynasty, and others. In each case, increasing complexity demanded increasing coordination costs, which were met by intensifying existing strategies rather than developing new integrative mechanisms — until the marginal cost of maintaining coherence exceeded the system's capacity to generate it. Tainter called this the "collapse of complex societies." CU provides the formal apparatus to explain why the pattern recurs: it is the inevitable consequence of CU-Ψ6 operating across timescales long enough for compensatory strategies to exhaust themselves.

4.2 Embodiment Loss: When Abstract Coherence Detaches

Section 3.5 introduced the vulnerability that the Axial revolution created: the possibility that abstract symbolic and normative coherence could detach from embodied, relational, and practical grounding. This section treats that detachment as a formal failure mode — one of the most common and consequential in civilizational history.

The mechanism is straightforward in CU terms. Abstract coherence — doctrinal systems, philosophical frameworks, legal codes, theological structures — achieves internal consistency through symbolic operations that do not require bodily practice, communal enactment, or direct experiential confirmation. When abstract coherence is integrated with embodied practice, each constrains the other: doctrine is tested against lived experience, and lived experience is organized by doctrine. The two coherence layers are coupled, and the coupling maintains the system's connection to reality (CU-C6: world-constrained coherence, applied at the social scale).

When the coupling weakens, abstract coherence becomes self-referential. It can still achieve high internal consistency — indeed, it often achieves *higher* internal consistency when freed from the messy constraints of embodied life. But that consistency is purchased at the cost of integration. CU-FP3 (Constraint Is Essential to Coherence) specifies the structural consequence: coherence without constraint collapses into fantasy. At the social scale, this manifests as symbolic systems that are logically rigorous but practically disconnected — theological frameworks that provide no guidance for suffering, legal systems that produce technical justice but substantive injustice, philosophical traditions that illuminate everything except how to live.

The institutional response to embodiment loss is characteristically compensatory: as internal integration declines, external enforcement increases. Inquisitions, loyalty oaths, ideological purity tests, and orthodoxy enforcement are not signs of strong coherence but of weak coherence — the system is attempting to maintain coordination through coercion because it can no longer maintain it through shared practice. CU-CL-5 (**Narrative Capture**) identifies the deepest form of this compensation: cultural systems that make dissent not merely forbidden but unintelligible — so that the very categories of thought available to participants exclude the possibility of questioning the framework.

Historical examples are abundant: late-stage Roman Christianity enforcing doctrinal uniformity while the experiential and communal grounding of early Christianity eroded; Confucian bureaucracies in late-imperial China enforcing examination orthodoxy while the living ethical practice that Confucius taught was reduced to rote memorization;

Soviet ideology enforcing materialist orthodoxy while the lived experience of citizens increasingly contradicted official narratives. In each case, the pattern is the same: symbolic coherence intensifies as embodied coherence declines, producing a system that is doctrinally rigid but experientially hollow.

4.3 Structural Collapse: When Embodiment Overwhelms Abstraction

The inverse failure mode is equally consequential, though less thoroughly analyzed in the existing literature.

Societies and movements that reject symbolic structure entirely — privileging spontaneity, authenticity, immediacy, or pure experience — often achieve extraordinary short-term vitality. Charismatic movements, cultural renaissances, and revolutionary upheavals generate intense shared coherence through embodied participation, emotional contagion, and the dissolution of rigid structures. The felt experience is one of liberation, authenticity, and collective effervescence.

But coherence without structure is fragile. Without symbolic memory (Rung 22), coherence cannot be stored across time. Without norms (Rung 24), coordination degrades beyond small-group scales. Without institutions (Rung 25), solutions to coordination problems must be reinvented rather than transmitted. The result is systems that are rich in affect but poor in persistence — movements that dissolve after a founder's death, communities that fragment under the first serious internal conflict, cultural moments that produce brilliant innovation but fail to institutionalize their insights.

In CU terms, this is coherence without constraint in the temporal dimension. The system achieves high C_c at a single moment but cannot maintain it across time because it lacks the structural mechanisms (norms, institutions, cultural memory) that provide temporal extension. CU-D6 (Multi-Timescale Coherence) specifies what is missing: slower integrative structures that constrain faster dynamics. Without them, the faster dynamics — emotional intensity, charismatic authority, collective excitement — dissipate as rapidly as they arose.

This failure mode appears in: the dissolution of charismatic religious movements after the death of their founders; the historical pattern in which tribal societies, however internally coherent, are absorbed or overwhelmed by less spontaneous but more structurally organized civilizations; the recurrent cycle in which artistic and cultural renaissances produce extraordinary creative output but fail to generate the institutional and normative frameworks necessary to preserve and extend their innovations; and the fate of revolutionary movements that successfully destroy existing structures but cannot construct viable alternatives.

The structural lesson is symmetrical: embodiment without abstraction is as unstable as abstraction without embodiment. Both extremes violate CU-FP3's requirement that coherence and constraint be co-present.

4.4 Fragmented Optimization: The Distinctly Modern Failure (CU-EC-2, CU-EC-6)

Modernity introduces a failure mode that is neither embodiment loss nor structural collapse but something more subtle: domain-specific hyper-coherence.

The modern world does not suffer from a shortage of coherence. Scientific disciplines achieve extraordinary internal consistency. Engineering systems achieve extraordinary precision. Financial instruments achieve extraordinary allocative efficiency. Legal systems achieve extraordinary procedural regularity. Each domain is, within its own boundaries, more coherent than anything pre-modern societies could have imagined.

The failure is that these domain-specific coherences are uncoupled from one another. Each subsystem optimizes within its own boundaries while externalizing costs to other subsystems, other timescales, and other scales of organization. In economic terms: growth metrics reward coherence extraction over creation (CU-EC-3), labor is valued for productivity rather than coherence contribution (CU-EC-4), capital concentrates without repair obligations (CU-EC-5), and repair costs are externalized rather than internalized (CU-EC-7, CU-EC-8). The result is a civilization of extraordinary parts and no functional whole — high local coherence, low global integration.

This is CU-Ψ6 at civilizational scale, and it operates through a specific mechanism: the progressive decoupling of the three coherence fields defined in Section 2.3. The individual field C_i, the cultural field C_c, and the ecological field C_e follow increasingly independent dynamics because the coupling mechanisms that once integrated them — shared practice, communal regulation, cultural meaning, religious cosmology — have been weakened by the very specialization that produced the domain-specific gains.

The consequences are paradoxical in a way that only CU-Ψ6 can explain:

Highly intelligent individuals are unable to find meaning — because intelligence operates within cognitive domains (high local C_i in the epistemic dimension) while meaning requires integration across domains (global C_i). Technologically advanced societies are unable to coordinate collective action — because technological capacity operates within engineering domains (high local C_c within technical systems) while coordination requires cross-domain integration (global C_c). Ethically sophisticated populations are unable to translate moral awareness into behavioral change — because ethical reasoning operates within normative domains (high local coherence in moral evaluation) while behavior change requires integration with motivation, identity, social context, and material conditions.

In each case, the same structural pattern: coherence within a domain, incoherence across domains. The system knows what to do but cannot do it, because the knowledge exists in one subsystem and the capacity for action exists in another, and the coupling between them has degraded.

4.5 Ideology as Compensatory Social Coherence

Ideology emerges at the point where integrative coherence fails. This claim, developed at the individual psychological level in Psychology §9.3 and at the group level in Psychology §10.5, operates with even greater force at the civilizational scale — and produces some of its most consequential effects there.

An ideology is not simply a false belief system. It is a top-down coherence prosthetic — a simplified narrative framework that provides moral certainty, identity anchoring, and explanatory closure in place of the unresolved complexity that integrative coherence would require. Ideologies are psychologically compelling because they solve a real problem: they reduce IES (CU-Ψ4) by providing structure where structure has collapsed, meaning where meaning has eroded, and belonging where belonging has been lost.

The structural signature of ideology, as opposed to genuine normative reasoning (Rungs 27–30), is that it achieves coherence through exclusion rather than integration. An ideology simplifies the coherence landscape by declaring certain regions of meaning space illegitimate — certain questions unaskable, certain experiences irrelevant, certain people unintelligible. This simplification reduces the coordination problem the system must solve, making large-scale alignment possible through shared narrative rather than genuine integration. But the simplification also violates CU-CL-11 (Narratives Must Permit Refusal): the excluded material does not disappear; it accumulates as suppressed incoherence that eventually destabilizes the system.

Both dominant modern political orientations exhibit this structure, though in characteristically different ways. What broadly counts as political liberalism tends to optimize individual-level coherence — personal autonomy, identity expression, freedom from constraint — while neglecting the social and ecological integration that makes individual flourishing sustainable across generations. What broadly counts as political conservatism tends to optimize social-level coherence — institutional stability, traditional authority, communal norms — while resisting the individual and systemic adaptation that changing conditions require.

Neither orientation is wrong in what it affirms. Each captures a genuine dimension of social coherence. Each becomes destructive when mistaken for a complete solution — when the partial coherence it provides is treated as sufficient, and the dimensions it excludes are dismissed as illegitimate. The CU diagnosis is that the polarization between them is itself a coherence failure: the inability to integrate individual and collective coherence within a single framework, resulting in oscillation between partial solutions rather than genuine synthesis.

4.6 Collapse as Regulatory Failure, Not Moral Failure

The failure modes described in this section share a structural feature that distinguishes the CU analysis from conventional historical explanation: none of them are primarily moral failures.

Systems do not collapse because people are evil, lazy, or stupid. They collapse because inherited coherence strategies are applied to conditions they were not designed for, because compensatory responses mask accumulating distortion, because feedback mechanisms degrade under the very pressures they were meant to detect, and because every coherence strategy has a domain of validity beyond which it converts from solution to problem.

This reframing matters practically, not merely theoretically. If collapse is primarily a moral failure, then the solution is moral improvement — better people, better values, stronger will. History provides no evidence that moral exhortation produces civilizational renewal. If collapse is a regulatory failure, then the solution is regulatory redesign — better coupling between coherence fields, better feedback mechanisms, better integration across scales and timescales. This is a design problem, not a virtue problem, and design problems admit of structural solutions.

CU-CL-6 (Culture as the Repair Layer) specifies the function that must be performed: when other systems fail, culture provides the repair mechanisms — rituals, narratives, and practices that restore coherence. The question for the present moment is whether the existing cultural repair layer is adequate to the scale of failure it must address — a question that Sections 5 and 5 take up directly.

4.7 Trauma as a Social-Scale Failure Mechanism

The failure modes described above operate at the level of institutions, ideologies, and structural incentives. But there is a deeper mechanism that drives social coherence collapse from within the agents themselves: psychological trauma.

Trauma, in Coherence Universalism terms, is not merely emotional distress. It is a constraint-level injury to an agent's coherence capacity — an experience that renders a previously viable mode of psychological organization unstable. The agent's set of psychologically viable interpretive states contracts. Formally, if V represents the set of stable cognitive-emotional configurations available to an individual, trauma acts as a constraint operator T such that $V' = T(V)$, where $V' \subset V$. The reduced space V' contains fewer stable interpretations of reality. When accurate representation of the world lies outside V', the individual cannot adopt it without destabilization. The result is not irrationality but constrained rationality: the system selects the most coherent interpretation available within its reduced viability region.

This produces defensive beliefs, projection, rigid identity formation, and threat sensitivity — patterns that are adaptive for the individual but corrosive to collective coherence.

The critical social-scale consequence follows from how humans stabilize coherence collectively. A group of agents each operating within restricted viability regions must find shared narratives stable for all participants. The collective viable region becomes the intersection of individual viability spaces: $V_{group} = \cap V'_i$. As trauma prevalence increases, this intersection shrinks. The group can no longer stabilize around nuanced or reality-tracking models, because those models require psychological states that some members cannot maintain. Instead, it stabilizes around simplified, emotionally safe attractors: binary moral framing, identity-protective reasoning, outgroup attribution of threat, and moral certainty with low predictive accuracy.

These are not communication failures — they are stability equilibria. Section 11 develops this mechanism in full, showing how trauma-driven viability contraction propagates through populations into institutional lock-in and civilizational-scale coherence degradation.

This section has identified three recurring failure modes across human history: embodiment loss (when abstract coherence detaches from practice), structural collapse (when material conditions overwhelm integrative capacity), and fragmented optimization (the distinctly modern failure, in which domain-specific coherence increases while cross-domain integration degrades). Each mode leaves characteristic signatures in individual psychology, institutional function, and cultural trajectory.

Section 5: Why Prior Solutions Cannot Scale Forward

If the present moment is a coherence crisis, the natural response is to reach for what has worked before. Why not return to religion, which generated extraordinary civilizational coherence for millennia? Why not double down on Enlightenment rationalism, which produced unprecedented scientific and technological progress? Why not strengthen liberal institutions, which enabled pluralism and individual flourishing? Why not revive national identity, which coordinated millions around shared purpose?

The short answer is that every historical coherence solution was tuned to a narrower constraint space than the one humanity now occupies. Each framework achieved genuine coherence within its domain — and each framework's domain of validity has been exceeded by conditions it was not designed to address.

What follows is not a critique of past frameworks. It is a structural explanation, grounded in the CU apparatus, of why each framework fails specific viability conditions under present constraints — and why no combination of past approaches, however cleverly assembled, can function as a primary integrator going forward.

5.1 Mythic-Religious Coherence: Powerful but Bounded

Premodern religious systems were among the most effective coherence technologies ever developed. They achieved what no other framework has matched: the simultaneous alignment of individual psychology (meaning, identity, moral regulation), social coordination (shared norms, communal practice, institutional authority), cosmological orientation (situating human life within a meaningful universe), and temporal extension (transmitting coherence across centuries through ritual, narrative, and institutional continuity).

In Ladder terms, religious systems occupied virtually every rung from embodied practice (Rungs 16–20) through shared representations and norms (Rungs 22–24) to institutions and culture (Rungs 25–26), with serious attempts at normative coherence (Rungs 27–30). They integrated bottom-up coherence (ritual, prayer, bodily discipline) with top-down coherence (doctrine, cosmology, ethical commandment) within a single framework. This integration is precisely what Section 4.2 identifies as the critical achievement — and its dissolution as the critical failure mode.

The limitation of mythic-religious coherence is not its depth but its structural assumptions. These systems function under conditions that no longer obtain at global scale:

Shared metaphysical commitment. Religious coherence depends on a population that shares, or can be induced to share, a common cosmological framework. In a globally interconnected, scientifically literate, religiously diverse world, no single metaphysical framework commands — or can command — universal assent. CU-CL-11 (Narratives Must Permit Refusal) specifies why this matters: coherence systems that cannot accommodate genuine dissent without rendering dissenters unintelligible become coercive. The history of religious coercion — inquisitions, forced conversions, heresy trials — is not an aberration of religious coherence but a structural consequence of extending a bounded coherence strategy beyond the population that shares its founding commitments.

Slow cultural transmission. Religious coherence was designed for environments in which meaning could be transmitted gradually, through childhood enculturation, communal practice, and intergenerational continuity. Modern conditions — information saturation, geographic mobility, exposure to competing frameworks from childhood — disrupt the slow transmission processes on which religious coherence depends. CU-D6 (Multi-Timescale Coherence) explains the problem: the timescale of religious cultural transmission (decades to centuries) is now radically mismatched with the timescale of informational and social change (months to years).

Resistance to epistemic revision. Religious frameworks are optimized for stability, not rapid adaptation. Their coherence depends partly on the continuity of foundational commitments — the very commitments that must remain stable if the framework is to provide the long-horizon meaning structure it was designed to supply. This stability is an asset under slow change and a liability under rapid change. When empirical evidence or changing social conditions require revision of foundational commitments, the framework faces a dilemma: revise and lose coherence, or resist revision and lose contact with reality. Both options degrade the system.

None of this means that religious traditions are without value. The embodied practices, communal structures, and existential wisdom they developed remain among the most sophisticated coherence technologies available. But they cannot function as the primary integrative framework for a planetary civilization characterized by pluralism, rapid change, and scientific literacy — not without becoming either coercive or diluted to the point of inefficacy.

5.2 Enlightenment Rationalism: Necessary but Insufficient

The Enlightenment was itself a coherence innovation — a response to the failure modes of mythic-religious systems described in Section 4.2. It correctly identified arbitrary authority, superstitious belief, and institutional corruption as coherence failures, and it proposed genuine solutions: empirical reasoning, constitutional governance, individual rights, the separation of church and state.

These contributions were real and remain necessary. No viable future framework can abandon the Enlightenment's core achievements: the commitment to evidence, the constraint of arbitrary power, the protection of individual conscience. In CU terms, the Enlightenment strengthened Rungs 27–30 (normative coherence) by subjecting inherited norms to rational scrutiny and developing principled methods for evaluating claims.

The failure mode lies in what the Enlightenment excluded. By attempting to ground coherence exclusively in reason and empirical fact, Enlightenment rationalism systematically weakened the coherence mechanisms it could not formalize:

Embodied regulation. Rationalism privileges propositional knowledge over embodied practice. It can explain why exercise reduces anxiety but cannot replace the coherence-generating function of communal dance. It can model social coordination but cannot replace the regulatory function of shared ritual. The lived, felt dimension of coherence — what Section 3.1 describes as the pre-symbolic foundation — falls outside the Enlightenment's epistemic frame, and what falls outside the frame is systematically devalued. The result is a civilization that understands coherence theoretically while progressively undermining the embodied practices through which coherence is actually generated.

Meaning generation. Rationalism can analyze meaning but cannot produce it. Meaning — the evaluative orientation that tells an agent what matters, what to pursue, and what to sacrifice for — is not derivable from empirical facts alone. The Enlightenment inherited its meaning structures from the religious traditions it critiqued (as Nietzsche observed with characteristic precision), and when those borrowed structures eroded, rationalism had no internal mechanism for replacing them. CU-CL-8 (Meaning Must Be Renewable) identifies the structural problem: a framework that can consume inherited meaning but not generate new meaning is operating on a depleting resource.

Consciousness and interiority. The Enlightenment's materialist metaphysics treated consciousness as epiphenomenal — a byproduct of physical processes rather than a structural feature of coherence. The Consciousness paper's analysis demonstrates why this is untenable: consciousness is not an add-on to coherence but the phenomenology of coherence under certain structural conditions (CF-1 through CF-5). A framework that dismisses consciousness as epiphenomenal cannot account for the felt dimension of meaning, identity, and value — and therefore cannot explain or address the meaning crisis it helped to create.

Rationalism can optimize systems. It cannot motivate humans at civilizational scale without borrowing meaning from frameworks it cannot itself generate. When stripped of those borrowings, it produces nihilism, technocracy, or value collapse — the conditions documented in Psychology §11.4 and elaborated in Section 6 of this paper.

5.3 Liberal Individualism: Local Coherence Without Global Integration

Modern liberalism excels at protecting individual autonomy. It allows diverse lifestyles, beliefs, and identities to coexist with minimal coordination costs. It has produced societies of extraordinary personal freedom and remarkable tolerance for difference — genuine coherence achievements at the individual and interpersonal scales.

Its structural limitation is that it optimizes C_i (individual coherence) without providing mechanisms for the maintenance of C_c (cultural coherence) or C_e (ecological coherence). When individuals optimize for personal coherence without integrative structures connecting individual choice to collective consequence, CU-Ψ6 operates with particular force:

each individual's locally rational choices aggregate into globally irrational outcomes.

Public goods erode because no individual has sufficient incentive to maintain them. Shared narratives dissolve because narrative construction is left to market forces that optimize for engagement rather than coherence (CU-CL-4: extractive cultures consume coherence). Responsibility diffuses because the connection between individual action and collective consequence is mediated by systems too complex for any individual to trace. The ecological field C_e degrades because the costs of individual consumption are externalized across timescales longer than any individual's planning horizon.

The result is a characteristic liberal paradox: societies that are psychologically permissive but structurally fragile. The system generates extraordinary individual flourishing under stable conditions — but precisely because it relies on external conditions remaining forgiving, it is vulnerable to perturbation in ways that more integrative (if less individually free) societies are not. When conditions worsen, liberalism lacks the cultural infrastructure (CU-CL-0) to coordinate a collective response, because it has systematically treated cultural coordination as a threat to individual autonomy rather than a precondition for its sustainability.

5.4 Nationalism and Ideological Movements: Emergency Coherence

Nationalist, revolutionary, and authoritarian movements restore social coherence through simplification. They reduce the complexity of the coordination problem by compressing identity into a single dimension (national, ethnic, ideological), establishing clear in-group/out-group boundaries, and providing moral certainty through binary narratives.

These strategies are not irrational. They are emergency coherence responses to conditions of acute fragmentation — the social-scale analog of the individual compensatory strategies described in Psychology §7.4. When shared meaning collapses and integrative frameworks fail, populations bifurcate into simplified coherence strategies because simplified coherence is better than no coherence at all. The psychology of radicalization (Psychology §10.5) operates identically at the civilizational scale.

The problem is that emergency coherence cannot sustain itself without escalation. Because ideological simplification achieves coherence through exclusion (Section 4.5), it requires perpetual conflict to maintain the boundary between in-group and out-group. Internal differentiation must be suppressed because it threatens the simplicity on which the framework's coherence depends. Nuance collapses into loyalty tests. And because the excluded complexity does not disappear — it accumulates as suppressed incoherence — the system must continually intensify its exclusionary mechanisms to maintain the same level of internal alignment.

In a technologically amplified world, these failure modes scale catastrophically. The authoritarian movements of the twentieth century — fascism, Stalinism, Maoism — demonstrated what happens when emergency coherence strategies are combined with industrial-scale enforcement capacity. The twenty-first century faces the same structural vulnerability with even greater amplification capacity: algorithmic polarization, surveillance technology, and AI-enabled propaganda can extend ideological coherence far more efficiently than any previous enforcement mechanism — which means that the failure modes, when they arrive, will be correspondingly more severe.

5.5 Postmodern Deconstruction: Diagnosis Without Repair

Postmodern critique made a genuine contribution to coherence analysis: it identified hidden power structures embedded in inherited meaning systems and demonstrated the contingency of frameworks that had been treated as natural or inevitable. In CU terms, postmodernism performed a diagnostic function — revealing the distortion (D(u)) concealed within apparently stable coherence structures, showing that what appeared as natural order was often historically constructed hierarchy.

The limitation is that deconstruction is a diagnostic tool, not a generative one. It can identify coherence failures but cannot construct coherence replacements. By dissolving inherited narratives without offering integrative alternatives, postmodernism produced a specific cultural condition: a population equipped with sophisticated tools for critique but no corresponding tools for construction.

CU-CL-6 (Culture as the Repair Layer) specifies what was missing: when existing coherence structures fail, culture must provide repair mechanisms — practices, narratives, and institutions that restore integration. Postmodern critique disabled the existing repair mechanisms (by demonstrating their contingency and embedded power relations) without developing new ones. The vacuum was filled by whatever coherence sources were available: market forces optimized for engagement, algorithms optimized for attention capture, and identity politics optimized for in-group solidarity — none of which satisfy the conditions for sustainable social coherence that the CU-CL principles specify.

5.6 Why Hybrids Fail

Many contemporary approaches attempt to hybridize past frameworks: science combined with spirituality, nationalism combined with market economics, liberalism combined with technocratic management, tradition combined with progressive values.

These hybrids fail when they stack incompatible coherence logics without resolving the tensions between them. Each historical framework has its own internal coherence structure — its own assumptions about what matters, how coordination works, and what counts as legitimate. When frameworks are combined without integrating their structural assumptions, the result is not synthesis but oscillation: the system swings between modes without settling into a stable configuration, because the frameworks provide contradictory guidance that the hybrid lacks the resources to reconcile.

In CU terms, these hybrids create multiple competing attractor basins within the same social coherence landscape, with no mechanism for navigating between them. The system does not integrate; it alternates — producing the characteristic modern experience of inconsistency between domains (scientifically rigorous at work, spiritually seeking on weekends; politically progressive in principle, economically conservative in practice) that registers psychologically as inauthenticity and culturally as fragmentation.

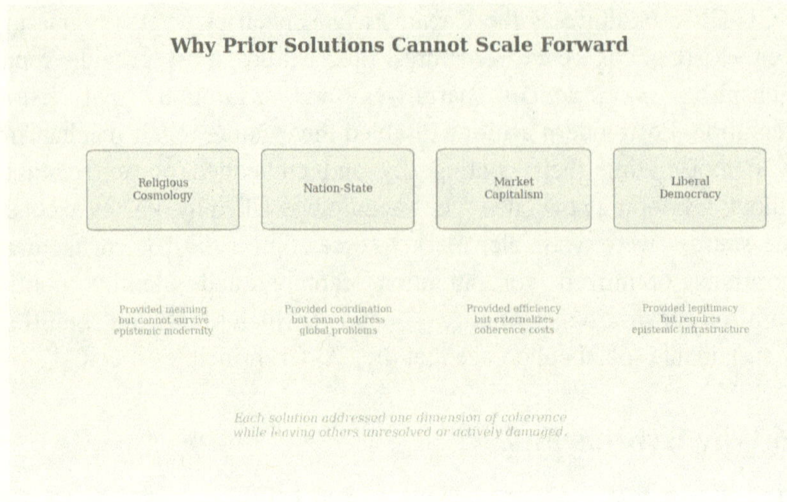

Figure 4. *Why prior solutions cannot scale forward. Each historical coherence strategy achieves coherence at certain scales while structurally failing at others. No single strategy addresses the full multi-scale integration the present crisis demands.*

5.7 The Shared Structural Limitation

Every historical coherence system operated under at least one of the following assumptions: a stable environment in which conditions change slowly relative to the system's adaptive capacity; a bounded population sharing enough common experience for shared meaning to emerge naturally; a common metaphysical worldview providing the foundational commitments around which coherence could be organized; slow rates of change allowing cultural transmission to keep pace with environmental novelty; and the possibility of externalizing consequences — dumping costs onto other populations, future generations, or ecological systems without immediate feedback.

None of these assumptions hold under present conditions. The environment is changing faster than any cultural system can adapt through inherited transmission mechanisms. The population is globally interconnected, sharing information but not meaning. No metaphysical framework commands universal assent. The rate of change continues to accelerate. And the era of externalization is ending: ecological limits, financial contagion, and informational cascades ensure that costs displaced in space or time return with compound interest.

What this analysis implies is not that past frameworks were wrong but that their validity was conditional on circumstances that no longer obtain. The constraint space has changed, and no framework designed for the old constraint space can serve as the primary integrator within the new one.

What is required is not a return but a framework capable of operating under present constraints: one that can generate coherence without requiring uniform belief, that can integrate across scales without requiring centralized control, that can adapt under rapid change without losing structural identity, and that can respect scientific rigor, ethical seriousness, and the felt dimension of meaning simultaneously.

Whether such a framework is possible, and what it would require, is the subject of Part II. But before turning to theory, the next section establishes the empirical conditions that any viable framework must address: the historically unprecedented convergence of multi-scale coherence failures that defines the present moment.

Section 6: The Present Crisis as a Coherence Bottleneck

Sections 3 through 4 established the historical trajectory: how social coherence was built across evolutionary and civilizational time, how it fails in characteristic patterns, and why no inherited framework can serve as the primary integrator under present conditions. This section brings the analysis to the present moment — not to repeat the psychological diagnosis already provided in Psychology §11.4, but to characterize the structural condition that makes the present crisis qualitatively different from previous civilizational disruptions.

The claim is precise: humanity is not merely experiencing rapid change, nor even a particularly severe civilizational downturn. It is encountering a **coherence bottleneck** — a structural condition in which existing coherence mechanisms cannot absorb the complexity now generated at biological, technological, social, and planetary scales simultaneously, and in which the traditional strategies for managing coherence pressure (slowing change, narrowing scope, enforcing uniformity, externalizing consequences) have all been foreclosed.

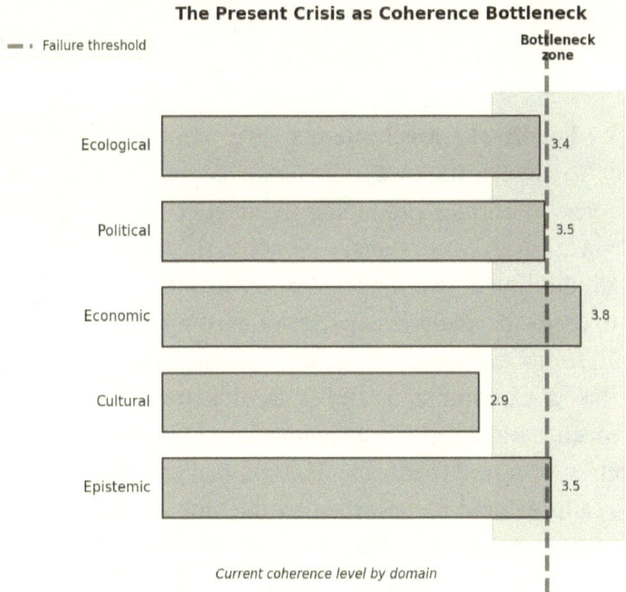

Figure 5. *The present crisis as a coherence bottleneck. Five domains — ecological, political, economic, cultural, and epistemic — simultaneously approach failure thresholds. The shaded region marks the bottleneck: a period in which all domains must be navigated simultaneously, with failure in any one capable of cascading into the others.*

6.1 What a Coherence Bottleneck Is

A coherence bottleneck is defined by the simultaneous satisfaction of three conditions:

Condition 1: The rate of novelty exceeds the system's integrative capacity. New information, new technologies, new social configurations, and new ecological pressures arrive faster than cultural coherence structures can absorb, evaluate, and integrate them. CU-D6 (Multi-Timescale Coherence) specifies the structural requirement: faster dynamics must be constrained by slower integrative structures. When faster dynamics outpace their integrative constraints, the system cannot regulate its own change — it is driven by novelty rather than navigating it.

Condition 2: Local coherence strategies undermine global stability. Subsystems optimize within their own domains in ways that degrade coherence at larger scales (CU-Ψ6). This is the defining pattern identified in Section 4.4 (fragmented optimization), but in a bottleneck it operates across all major domains simultaneously rather than in isolated sectors.

Condition 3: Feedback mechanisms are compromised. The system's capacity to detect its own coherence degradation has been weakened by the very dynamics producing the degradation — information overload drowns diagnostic signals in noise, institutional distrust undermines the credibility of warning systems, and the complexity of causal pathways exceeds the analytic capacity of existing frameworks.

Previous civilizations encountered subsets of these conditions. The Roman Empire faced Conditions 1 and 2 as it expanded beyond its administrative capacity. Medieval Christendom faced Conditions 2 and 3 as doctrinal rigidity suppressed feedback. The colonial era faced all three, but regionally — failure could be absorbed by the global system because not all regions were simultaneously affected.

The present bottleneck is historically unique because all three conditions are satisfied globally and simultaneously, with no external buffer to absorb failure.

6.2 The Five Domains of Simultaneous Failure

The bottleneck manifests across five interacting domains. The Introduction (§1.5) previewed these; this section develops the structural analysis.

6.2.1 Scale Mismatch

The defining structural feature of the present moment is the mismatch between the scale at which problems operate and the scale at which human coherence mechanisms were designed to function.

Human cognition evolved for small-group coordination in environments characterized by local causation, direct feedback, and relatively stable conditions (Section 3.1; Dunbar, 1992). These cognitive capacities are now embedded in planetary systems where causation is distributed, feedback is delayed or mediated by complex intermediary systems, and conditions change faster than embodied intuition can track. The result is a systematic mismatch between the scale of consequences and the scale of comprehension.

Institutions face the same mismatch. Governance structures designed for bounded populations operating under relatively stable conditions — the nation-state, the regulatory agency, the international treaty — are attempting to manage nonlinear, rapidly evolving dynamics that cross every boundary they were designed to patrol. Climate change, financial contagion, pandemic risk, algorithmic disruption, and AI development all operate at scales and speeds that exceed the regulatory capacity of institutions designed for slower, more local, more predictable conditions.

In CU terms, the coherence gradient has steepened beyond the system's regulatory bandwidth. The problems are real and their solutions are structurally available — but the coupling mechanisms that would connect understanding to action, diagnosis to intervention, local capacity to global need, have not kept pace with the problems they must address.

6.2.2 The Collapse of Shared Meaning Infrastructure

Section 3.4 described how the shared meaning fields that historically aligned individual motivation with collective action — religious cosmologies, mythic narratives, national stories, ethical traditions — were progressively weakened by the forces of modernity. Section 5.7 established that no prior framework can replace them under present conditions.

The consequence is a population that must construct meaning individually from incompatible sources. Scientific worldviews provide causal explanation but no evaluative orientation. Moral intuitions provide evaluative orientation but no metaphysical grounding. Political identities provide belonging but without shared models of reality. Consumer culture provides stimulation but without integration. Each source provides genuine coherence within its own dimension while failing to connect to the others — the fragmented optimization of Section 4.4 operating at the level of individual meaning construction.

CU-CL-8 (Meaning Must Be Renewable) identifies the structural problem: the modern world consumes inherited meaning faster than it produces new meaning. The religious and cultural traditions that once renewed meaning through ritual, narrative, and communal practice have weakened; the institutions that replaced them — market, media, state — optimize for engagement, efficiency, or compliance rather than meaning generation. The result is a population experiencing what Vervaeke (2019) calls "the meaning crisis" — not an absence of information but an absence of integration, not a shortage of options but a shortage of frameworks within which options become meaningful.

6.2.3 Information Overload as Coherence Saturation

Information abundance does not automatically produce understanding. Beyond a threshold determined by the system's integrative capacity, additional information degrades coherence rather than enhancing it.

The modern media environment — and particularly the attention economy built on algorithmic optimization — saturates attention with novelty while systematically undermining the conditions required for integration. Meaning requires duration, repetition, and embodied engagement (Section 3.1; CU-D6). The attention economy — which treats attention as an extractable resource rather than a scarce coherence input (CU-EC-10) — optimizes for interruption, novelty, and emotional salience — precisely the conditions that prevent temporal integration. The result is a population that is maximally informed and minimally integrated: aware of more problems than any previous generation, capable of sustained response to fewer of them.

This produces a distinctive psychological and social profile: high stimulation with low integration; moral outrage without sustained action; identity volatility driven by exposure to incompatible frameworks; and chronic anxiety arising not from any specific threat but from the system's inability to organize its informational environment into a coherent whole. From a systems perspective, this is coherence noise overwhelming signal — the informational equivalent of the feedback degradation identified in Condition 3 of the bottleneck definition.

6.2.4 Polarization as Failed Coherence Repair

Polarization is routinely framed as a moral or ideological conflict — a battle between competing values that could be resolved if one side would yield or if both sides could compromise. The CU analysis reframes it as a failed attempt at coherence repair.

When shared meaning infrastructure collapses (§6.2.2) and integrative capacity is overwhelmed (§6.2.3), populations bifurcate into simplified coherence strategies. Each faction restores internal order — in-group solidarity, moral clarity, identity stability — by externalizing incoherence onto the opposing faction. The other side becomes the repository of everything the in-group cannot integrate: the cause of the problems, the obstacle to solutions, the embodiment of what is wrong with the world. This is CU-Ψ6 operating through the mechanism of ideology described in Section 4.5: local coherence is purchased through exclusion, and the excluded material is projected onto the out-group.

This structural analysis explains several features of modern polarization that are otherwise puzzling. It explains why polarization intensifies precisely when cooperation is most needed — because the conditions that demand cooperation (complexity, uncertainty, shared vulnerability) are the same conditions that overwhelm integrative capacity and trigger compensatory simplification. It explains why moral arguments cannot resolve polarization — because polarization is not a moral disagreement but a regulatory failure, and moral arguments are processed within the already-polarized framework rather than operating on the framework itself. And it explains why exposure to opposing views often increases polarization rather than reducing it (as empirical research consistently demonstrates) — because the opposing view is experienced not as information to be integrated but as a threat to the coherence that the polarized framework provides.

6.2.5 Technology as Coherence Amplifier

Technology is not the origin of the coherence crisis. The structural dynamics described in this paper — scale mismatch, embodiment loss, fragmented optimization, ideological compensation — all predate digital technology by decades or centuries. But technology dramatically accelerates every one of them.

Artificial intelligence, social media, and algorithmic optimization magnify existing coherence gradients without providing integrative regulation. Social media algorithms optimize for engagement — which, given human psychology, means optimizing for emotional salience, conflict, and in-group solidarity — producing an information environment that systematically amplifies CU-Ψ6 (local—global tension) at the population level. AI systems optimize within their objective functions with extraordinary efficiency while externalizing costs to domains their objective functions do not represent — fragmented optimization (Section 4.4) operating at machine speed. Surveillance and persuasion technologies extend the reach of ideological coherence strategies (Section 4.5) far beyond what any pre-digital enforcement mechanism could achieve.

The danger is not that technology will replace humanity. It is that technology will outpace humanity's capacity to remain coherent — amplifying agency without amplifying the integrative wisdom that determines whether amplified agency produces flourishing or catastrophe. This is the theme that *CU — Artificial Intelligence* will develop in detail.

6.3 Why This Bottleneck Cannot Be Bypassed

Previous coherence crises were resolved through one or more of three strategies: slowing change (through isolation, conservatism, or deliberate simplification), narrowing scope (through specialization, boundary-drawing, or ignoring what could not be addressed), or externalizing consequences (through colonization, resource extraction from peripheral populations, or deferral to future generations).

None of these strategies remain available at the scale required.

Change cannot be slowed because the drivers of acceleration — technological development, information proliferation, ecological feedback — are self-reinforcing and globally distributed. No single society can opt out without being overwhelmed by the dynamics it refuses to engage.

Scope cannot be narrowed because the problems are globally coupled. Climate change, pandemic risk, financial contagion, AI development, and nuclear proliferation do not respect the boundaries within which scope-narrowing operates. A nation that ignores climate change does not avoid its consequences; it merely loses the capacity to influence them.

Consequences cannot be externalized because the era of externalization is ending. Ecological limits ensure that costs displaced onto the biosphere return as resource constraint and environmental disruption. Financial interconnection ensures that costs displaced onto other economies return as contagion. Informational transparency ensures that costs displaced onto other populations return as political instability and migration.

The bottleneck must be passed through. The question is not whether humanity will change but how — whether the reorganization will be navigated or merely suffered, whether it will produce higher-order integration or merely a new configuration of fragmentation.

6.4 The Bottleneck as Phase Transition

A structural observation, drawn from the dynamics principles, provides a measure of hope within this diagnosis.

Bottlenecks are not only points of failure. They are points of phase transition — moments at which the system's existing configuration is destabilized sufficiently that reorganization around deeper attractors becomes possible. CU-D5 (Non-Equilibrium Stability) specifies that coherent systems are stable far from equilibrium, maintained by continuous energy throughput rather than resting at minimal states. Phase transitions occur when the system's existing far-from-equilibrium configuration becomes unsustainable and the system must reorganize or collapse.

At such moments, new organizing principles become possible that were inaccessible from the previous stable configuration — just as the Axial revolution (Section 3.5) was possible only because the pre-Axial coherence structures had been destabilized, and just as the scientific revolution was possible only because medieval coherence structures had been strained beyond recovery. The same forces that make collapse possible also make transformation structurally available.

The present bottleneck makes visible, for the first time at civilizational scale, the dynamics that have always governed social coherence but were previously operable only implicitly — through inherited practice, unreflective tradition, and cultural inertia. The crisis of coherence is simultaneously the opportunity to become coherence-aware: to understand the structures that sustain integration, the thresholds at which they fail, and the conditions under which they can be deliberately cultivated across scales.

6.5 The Transition to Part II

Part I has established three conclusions:

First, human history is a coherence trajectory — a sequence of strategies for generating, stabilizing, and transmitting integration across expanding scales — and each strategy carries characteristic tradeoffs and failure modes that are structurally predictable through the CU apparatus (Section 3).

Second, these failure modes follow recurrent patterns — embodiment loss, structural collapse, fragmented optimization, ideological compensation — that are applications of CU-Ψ6, CU-FP3, CU-D6, and CU-CL principles at the civilizational scale (Section 4).

Third, no prior coherence framework can function as the primary integrator under present conditions, because the constraint space has changed beyond the validity domain of every inherited strategy (Section 4), and the resulting convergence of multi-scale failures constitutes a bottleneck that cannot be bypassed through the traditional mechanisms of slowing, narrowing, or externalizing (this section).

Part II turns from diagnosis to theory: the formal analysis of multi--scale coherence dynamics, the structures through which social coherence is generated and maintained, the thresholds at which it fails, and the conditions under which it can be restored. The task is not to prescribe a future ideology but to describe the structural conditions under which many futures remain possible — the conditions under which coherence can be generated without coercion, maintained without rigidity, and transmitted without exclusion.

This section has argued that the present crisis is not merely rapid change but a coherence bottleneck: the simultaneous approach of failure thresholds in ecological, political, economic, cultural, and epistemic domains. Unlike previous crises, the bottleneck requires all domains to be navigated simultaneously, with failure in any one capable of cascading into the others. Part II turns from diagnosis to theory.

Part II — Toward Social Coherence Theory

Section 7: Multi-Scale Coherence Dynamics

Part I established the historical diagnosis: how social coherence has been generated and lost across civilizational time, why inherited coherence strategies cannot scale forward, and why the present moment constitutes a structural bottleneck. Part II turns from diagnosis to theory — the formal analysis of how coherence operates across multiple interacting scales, what structural conditions determine whether it holds or collapses, and what follows for intervention and design.

This section develops the paper's primary formal contribution: the analysis of multi-field coherence coupling. Where the Psychology paper formalized how coherence operates within an individual system — introducing C(u), D(u), V, FCS, IES, and the CU-Ψ principles — this section formalizes how coherence operates between systems at different scales, and why the coupling between scales is where most civilizational-level coherence dynamics actually play out.

7.1 From Implicit to Explicit Coherence Management

Every society manages coherence. No society has explicitly understood that this is what it is doing.

Historically, coherence was generated implicitly — through shared myth, ritual synchronization, moral uniformity, geographic isolation, and slow rates of change (Section 3). These mechanisms worked because complexity remained within bounds that implicit management could handle. A village elder did not need a theory of coherence to maintain social integration; the practices themselves, accumulated across generations, performed the integrative function.

Modern conditions break this assumption (Section 6). When systems exceed intuitive integration limits, when multiple value systems coexist without a shared grammar, when change outpaces traditional transmission, and when power is distributed across scales that no individual or community can manage — then coherence management must become explicit. Not in the sense of centralized control, which is itself a coherence failure mode (Section 4.2), but in the sense of structural understanding: knowing what coherence is, how it operates across scales, where it is degrading, and what conditions must be satisfied for it to be restored.

This is the transition that CU proposes: from coherence as something that happens to societies (maintained by inheritance, disrupted by change) to coherence as something that societies can understand and cultivate (analyzed through formal principles, diagnosed through structural indicators, supported through deliberate design). The remainder of Part II develops the framework that makes this transition possible.

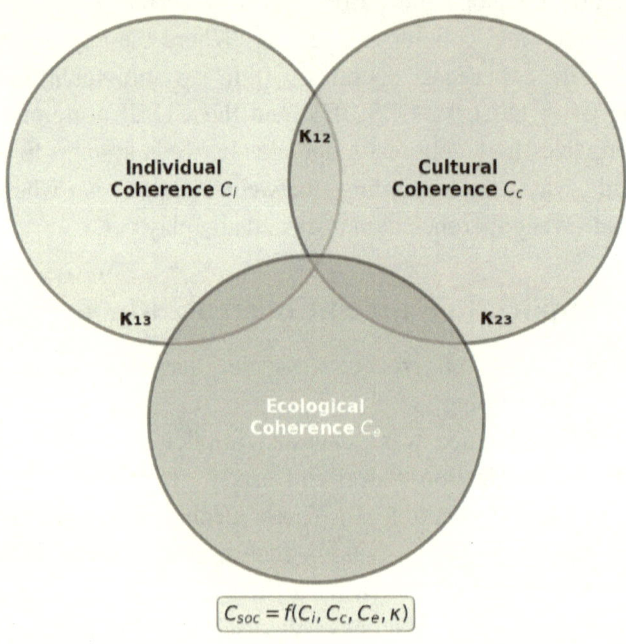

Figure 6. *The three-field coupling model. Social coherence C_soc emerges from the interaction of three fields: individual coherence C_i, cultural coherence C_c, and ecological coherence C_e, coupled by parameters κ. No single field determines social coherence; it is the coupling structure that matters.*

7.2 Why Single-Scale Models Fail

The most important structural insight of this paper — and the one most frequently violated in both academic analysis and policy design — is that coherence cannot be understood or maintained at a single scale.

A single-scale model implicitly assumes that coherence gradients are locally generated and locally regulated: that an individual's coherence depends primarily on individual-level processes, that a culture's coherence depends primarily on cultural-level processes, that ecological stability depends primarily on ecological-level processes. This assumption is false in every real system.

The empirical counterexamples are decisive:

An individual may achieve high internal coherence — strong identity, clear values, effective self-regulation — and still suffer in a fragmented culture that provides no distributed regulatory support, no shared meaning infrastructure, and no stable institutional context for sustained action. The Psychology paper documented this: individual FCS (CU-Ψ3) depends partly on the shared coherence fields (CU-Ψ12) in which the individual is embedded. Therapy that raises individual coherence within a degraded cultural field produces gains that are real but fragile — the individual must continuously self-regulate what a healthier culture would co-regulate, a burden that eventually exhausts even well-functioning systems (Psychology, Appendix H).

A culture may achieve high internal coherence — strong institutions, shared norms, effective coordination — and still collapse under ecological stress that undermines the material conditions on which cultural functioning depends. Historical examples are numerous: Diamond (1997) documented civilizational collapses driven by ecological degradation in societies that maintained strong internal cultural coherence up to the point of environmental failure.

An ecological system may be fundamentally stable but suffer degradation driven by cultural practices that extract resources faster than regeneration allows. The ecological system's "coherence" — its capacity for self-regulation and renewal — is compromised not by internal dynamics but by external pressure from a cultural field operating on a different timescale with different optimization criteria.

In every case, the failure is at the interface between scales, not within any single scale. Social coherence is non-reductive (CU-FP5): it cannot be decomposed into individual-level processes without losing the coupling dynamics that determine collective outcomes. This is CU-D9 (The Multi-Scale Failure Principle) in action: coherence fails through cross-scale conflict, temporal misalignment, and cascade collapse. Understanding these dynamics requires modeling the coupling between scales explicitly.

7.3 The Three Coherence Fields and Their Coupling

Section 2.3 introduced the three coherence fields — individual (C_i), cultural (C_c), and ecological (C_e). We now formalize how they interact.

7.3.1 The Individual Field (C_i)

The individual field encompasses everything the Psychology paper analyzed: cognitive, emotional, motivational, identity-level, and embodied coherence. Its formal characterization is provided by the CU-Ψ apparatus — C(u) on state space H, the viability region V, FCS and IES as aggregate measures, the meaning map Φ, and the coherence drive (CU-Ψ5, the psychological instantiation of CU-D2) that governs the system's sensitivity to coherence gradients.

What this paper adds is the recognition that C_i is not a closed system. Key parameters of individual coherence — the breadth of V, the baseline level of IES, the availability of regulatory resources, the content of the meaning map — depend on the cultural field C_c in which the individual is embedded. The individual's viability region V_i is not fixed by individual psychology alone; it is partly constituted by the cultural infrastructure available to the individual. A person embedded in a supportive community with strong relational bonds, meaningful work, and stable institutional context has a broader effective V_i — a larger range of conditions under which identity-preserving functioning is possible — than the same person in isolation or in a fragmented social field.

This dependence operates through the shared coherence fields (CU-Ψ12) described in Psychology §9. Shared coherence fields distribute regulatory burden: they provide the coordination, meaning infrastructure, and relational support that reduce the load on individual self-regulation. When shared coherence fields are strong, individual IES is lower because much of the regulatory work is being performed by the distributed field rather than by the individual alone. When shared coherence fields weaken, individual IES rises because the individual must now self-regulate what was previously co-regulated — a structural explanation for why the decline of communal institutions produces population-level increases in anxiety, depression, and meaning loss (Psychology §11.4).

7.3.2 The Cultural Field (C_c)

The cultural field encompasses the coherence of shared representations (Rung 22), coordination dynamics (Rung 23), norms (Rung 24), institutions (Rung 25), and culture (Rung 26). Its dynamics are governed by the CU-CL principles and the institutional principles CU-Inst-0 through CU-Inst-8.

C_c is the primary subject of this paper. Its formal characterization requires concepts that extend beyond the individual-level apparatus:

Institutional coherence is the degree to which a society's formal institutions — legal systems, governance structures, educational systems, economic frameworks — satisfy the institutional principles. CU-Inst-0 (Institutional Legitimacy) specifies that institutions are coherence technologies whose legitimacy depends on preserving the coherence of those they organize. CU-Inst-4 (Scale Alignment) specifies that institutional scale must match the scale of problems addressed. CU-Inst-8 (Evolutionary Revisability) specifies that institutions must be capable of revision in response to changing conditions. When these conditions are satisfied, institutions contribute to C_c by stabilizing coordination across time and scale. When they are violated, institutions become sources of cultural incoherence — rigidified structures that consume coordination resources while failing to produce the coordination benefits that justify their existence.

Normative coherence is the degree to which a society's norms are mutually compatible, well-adapted to current conditions, and supported by both institutional enforcement and embodied practice. Normative incoherence — a condition in which a society's explicit norms contradict its actual practices, or in which competing norm systems operate without mechanisms for resolution — is among the most psychologically destabilizing features of modern life, because it places the burden of reconciling incompatible demands on individuals who lack the resources to resolve what is structurally unresolvable at the individual scale.

Symbolic coherence is the degree to which a society's shared meaning infrastructure — narratives, values, cultural practices, aesthetic forms — provides its members with frameworks adequate for orienting action, constructing identity, and generating purpose. CU-CL-3 (Coherence Creation) specifies that healthy cultures create coherence; CU-CL-4 (**Coherence Extraction**) specifies that extractive cultures consume it. The distinction is not between content (which narratives, which values) but function (does the symbolic infrastructure generate more coherence than it consumes, or does it deplete the coherence of its participants?).

C_c depends on C_i in a specific and important way: cultural coherence is not maintained by abstract structures alone but by the participation of individuals who enact, transmit, and revise cultural content. A culture's norms are stable only insofar as individuals internalize and practice them. Its institutions function only insofar as individuals occupy roles within them with sufficient competence and commitment. Its symbolic infrastructure persists only insofar as individuals find it meaningful enough to transmit. Cultural coherence that is maintained purely through enforcement, without individual internalization, is already exhibiting the compensatory dynamics of Section 4.2 — and is structurally fragile.

7.3.3 The Ecological Field (C_e)

The ecological field encompasses the coherence of environmental, material, and planetary systems. C_e operates on the longest timescales of any coherence field — decades to millennia — and with the highest inertia. Changes in C_e are slow to manifest but difficult or impossible to reverse once they cross critical thresholds.

C_e enters this paper primarily as a boundary condition and coupling term. Its full formal treatment awaits a future paper. But its inclusion is essential for two reasons.

First, ecological coherence constrains the long-term viability of everything built upon it. No cultural achievement persists if the material conditions that support it are undermined. The most sophisticated institutional framework is irrelevant if the ecological base that sustains the population degrades beyond recovery. C_e sets an absolute bound on the long-term viability of C_c and C_i — a constraint that is easily ignored in the short term (because ecological timescales are longer than political or economic timescales) but ultimately non-negotiable.

Second, the coupling between C_c and C_e is where some of the most consequential dynamics of the present crisis operate. Cultural practices that extract resources faster than ecological renewal permits are, in CU terms, cultural systems that consume ecological coherence to maintain cultural coherence — the extractive dynamic of CU-CL-4 operating across the C_c/C_e interface. The ecological consequences are delayed by the long timescales of C_e, but they are cumulative and, beyond certain thresholds, irreversible.

7.4 The Coupling Structure: Bidirectional but Asymmetric

The central formal claim of multi-field coherence theory is that the three fields are coupled: each field's dynamics depend on the states of the others. But the coupling is not symmetric. It exhibits a characteristic asymmetry that has profound implications for both diagnosis and intervention.

Downward coupling is faster and stronger than upward coupling. When C_c degrades, the effects on C_i are rapid and severe: individuals lose distributed regulatory support, IES rises, meaning infrastructure collapses, and the population experiences the psychological consequences documented in Psychology §11.4. When C_e degrades, the effects on C_c are delayed but ultimately overwhelming: ecological stress undermines the material basis for institutional functioning, cultural transmission, and long-term planning.

Upward coupling is slower and more diffuse. Individual coherence improvements (higher FCS, reduced IES, expanded integrative capacity) benefit C_c only to the extent that they are aggregated and institutionalized — a process that requires meso-scale structures (Section 8) and operates on timescales of years to decades. Cultural coherence improvements benefit C_e only to the extent that they change the aggregate pattern of material extraction — a process that operates on timescales of decades to centuries.

This asymmetry has a practical consequence that Section 4.6 stated as a general principle and this section makes formally precise: **destruction propagates downward faster than repair propagates upward.** Ecological degradation produces cultural instability more quickly than cultural reform produces ecological recovery. Cultural fragmentation produces individual suffering more quickly than individual healing produces cultural renewal. This is why cascading collapse is the characteristic failure mode of multi-field systems (Section 7.5), and why repair requires deliberate scaffolding across scales rather than the expectation that improvement at one level will spontaneously propagate to others.

The coupling also operates through different mechanisms at each interface:

$C_c \rightarrow C_i$ coupling operates through shared coherence fields (CU-Ψ12): the norms, institutions, narratives, and relational structures that provide distributed regulation for individual coherence. When these structures are strong, individuals receive regulatory support that broadens their effective viability region. When they weaken, individuals must self-regulate what was previously co-regulated — producing the population-level increases in psychological distress that characterize periods of cultural fragmentation.

$C_i \rightarrow C_c$ coupling operates through participation, innovation, and critique: the aggregate contribution of individuals to the maintenance and revision of cultural structures. This coupling is weaker and slower because cultural change requires coordination across many individuals, whereas individual impact from cultural change is immediate and direct. However, under certain conditions — the presence of effective meso-scale structures (Section 8), the alignment of individual innovation with institutional capacity for absorption, the availability of cultural mechanisms for integrating novelty — upward coupling can be sufficient to produce genuine cultural renewal.

$C_c \rightarrow C_e$ coupling operates through the aggregate material impact of cultural practices: resource extraction, land use, pollution, energy consumption, and the institutional frameworks that regulate (or fail to regulate) these practices. This coupling is currently pathological: modern cultural systems extract ecological coherence at rates that exceed regeneration, producing the slow-building ecological crisis that constrains long-term viability.

$C_e \rightarrow C_c$ coupling operates through material constraint: ecological degradation undermines the resource base, climate stability, and environmental predictability on which cultural functioning depends. This coupling is delayed by C_e's high inertia but is, beyond certain thresholds, catastrophic and irreversible.

7.5 Cascade Dynamics

Multi-field coupling introduces the possibility of cascade collapse — a process in which coherence failure at one scale propagates across scales, each failure amplifying the next.

CU-D9 (The Multi-Scale Failure Principle) identifies cascade collapse as one of the characteristic multi-scale failure patterns. The multi-field framework makes it formally precise.

Downward cascade. Ecological degradation (C_e declining) constrains the material conditions for institutional functioning → institutional instability raises the IES of cultural systems (C_c declining) → cultural fragmentation weakens the distributed regulatory support available to individuals → individual coherence degrades (C_i declining), producing population-level psychological distress. Each stage amplifies the next because the degraded field can no longer buffer the fields below it.

Compensatory cascade. When a higher-level field degrades, lower-level fields may compensate by intensifying their own coherence maintenance — but compensation has limits and costs. Individuals in a fragmenting culture may intensify personal meaning-seeking (high coherence drive, CU-Ψ5), but without cultural scaffolding, the intensification risks producing the dysregulated patterns described in Psychology §7.4 — anxiety, compulsive behavior, ideological capture. Communities in an unstable institutional environment may intensify in-group solidarity, but without institutional mediation, the intensification risks producing the polarization dynamics of Section 5.2.4. Compensation is real and sometimes necessary, but it is a survival strategy, not a sustainable equilibrium.

Upward cascade (rare but possible). Under specific structural conditions — when meso-scale structures provide effective mediation, when cultural institutions are capable of absorbing innovation (CU-Inst-8), and when the higher-level field has not crossed irreversible thresholds — improvements at lower levels can propagate upward. A critical mass of individually coherent agents, organized through effective meso-scale structures, can revitalize cultural institutions. Renewed cultural practices can shift the aggregate material impact on ecological systems. These upward cascades are the structural basis for civilizational renewal — but they require deliberate scaffolding and cannot be relied upon to occur spontaneously.

7.6 The Cross-Scale Coherence Constraint

The preceding analysis yields a formal constraint that any viable social system must satisfy:

Proposition 6.1 (Cross-Scale Viability Constraint). A multi-field system remains globally viable only if, at every level $\ell \in \{i, c, e\}$:

\(a\) The distortion D(u) at level ℓ remains within the viability region V_ℓ — that is, the accumulated incoherence at each scale does not exceed the scale's capacity for self-regulation and repair.

\(b\) The viability of each level is not being maintained by extracting coherence from adjacent levels faster than those levels can regenerate — that is, CU-CL-4 (coherence extraction) is not operating across the interfaces between fields.

\(c\) Higher-scale coherence enables rather than suppresses lower-scale coherence — that is, cultural coherence supports rather than constrains individual flourishing (CU-Inst-1: Local Agency Preservation), and ecological coherence provides rather than withdraws the material conditions for cultural functioning.

When all three conditions are satisfied, the system exhibits sustainable multi-scale coherence: each field operates within its viability region, the coupling between fields is generative rather than extractive, and the system can absorb perturbation without cascade collapse.

When any condition is violated, the system is operating on borrowed time. The violation may be masked by compensatory dynamics (Section 6.5), by the temporal lag between cause and effect across coupling interfaces, or by the sheer inertia of higher-level fields. But the violation accumulates, and unless corrected, eventually produces the cascade failures that Section 9 will formalize as explicit thresholds.

7.7 Implications

This analysis explains, with structural precision, why so many well-intentioned interventions fail:

Individual therapy is insufficient not because therapy is ineffective but because individual coherence depends partly on cultural coherence ($C_c \rightarrow C_i$ coupling), and therapy alone cannot repair a degraded cultural field. The gains are real but fragile — maintained against the current of a cultural environment that continuously generates the very distress therapy is attempting to treat.

Political reform is insufficient not because policy is irrelevant but because institutional change alone cannot restore cultural coherence when the normative and symbolic infrastructure on which institutions depend has degraded. Policy without cultural renewal is enforcement without legitimacy — the compensatory dynamic of Section 4.2 applied to governance.

Spiritual practice is insufficient not because contemplative insight is illusory but because individual insight without structural support collapses under the pressure of re-engagement with a fragmented world. The insight is real; its integration requires conditions that no individual practice can provide alone.

Ecological policy is insufficient not because environmental regulation is unnecessary but because ecological coherence depends on cultural practices that ecological policy alone cannot change. Regulation that constrains behavior without changing the cultural meaning-systems that motivate behavior produces compliance without transformation — a gap that eventually undermines the regulation itself.

Each intervention addresses one field while presupposing the stability of the others. None addresses the coupling between fields — the interface dynamics where the most consequential failures occur and where the highest-leverage interventions would operate.

Sections 7.8 and 6.9 formalize these qualitative dynamics through the social coherence functional — a composite measure that makes the multi-scale analysis amenable to precise dynamical modeling. The remainder of Part II then develops the structures through which cross-scale coherence can be built: the meso-scale intermediaries that mediate between individual and cultural fields (Section 8), the formal thresholds at which coupling fails (Section 9), the design principles for interventions that operate across scales rather than within them (Section 10), and the trauma-cascade dynamics that drive downward coherence regimes (Section 11).

7.8 Formalizing Social Coherence: The Social Coherence Functional

The preceding sections described multi-scale coherence dynamics qualitatively — three coupled fields, bidirectional asymmetric coupling, cascade propagation. This section introduces a formal object that makes these dynamics amenable to precise analysis: the social coherence functional.

Let a society at time t be described by a macrostate x_t that bundles measurable, coarse-grained variables: institutional trust, violence rate, inequality, information integrity, polarization, coordination capacity, ecological load, and innovation rate. Let there be N agents, each with an internal state $m_i(t)$ (beliefs, values, predictive model) and actions $a_i(t)$. The macrostate x_t is a coarse-graining of these individual states and the environment.

Define a social coherence functional $C_{soc}(x)$, the social-scale instantiation of the general coherence functional C(x) developed in the Physics and Biology papers, intended to summarize how well the system maintains integration under constraint. Following the Biology paper's treatment of organismic coherence, where adequacy is defined as a geometric mean so that the collapse of any single viability constraint collapses the whole, we adopt a multiplicative form:

$$C_{soc}(x) = (T(x) \cdot I(x) \cdot K(x) \cdot R(x))^{(1/4)} \cdot e^{(-\lambda \cdot E(x))}$$

where the four positive components — each normalized to [0, 1] — enter as a geometric mean, and extraction E(x) acts as a multiplicative suppressor rather than a linearly subtracted term. The geometric mean enforces a crucial structural property: if any single pillar drops to zero, social coherence collapses regardless of the strength of the remaining components. A society with perfect coordination but zero trust is not "three-quarters coherent" — it is structurally inviable, just as a cell with zero ATP production is dead regardless of its membrane integrity. The extraction term $e^{(-\lambda E)}$ ensures that externalized harm degrades the entire system rather than being offset by gains elsewhere, consistent with the Local—Global Coherence Principle. The parameter $\lambda > 0$ controls the sensitivity of coherence to extraction.

The five components correspond to measurable dimensions of social coherence:

T(x): Trust and predictive reliability. Agents can anticipate each other's behavior; deception is low; social interactions are low-friction and predictable. Possible empirical proxies include generalized social trust surveys, perceived institutional fairness and legitimacy, contract reliability indices, and interpersonal violence rates (inverse). This connects to the interpersonal predictability dimension of social coherence described in Section 2 and the coordination norms of Rungs 23–25 on the Coherence Ladder.

I(x): Information integrity. The epistemic environment enables shared reality. Signal exceeds noise; epistemic institutions function. Proxies include misinformation prevalence, epistemic polarization metrics (disagreement about basic facts), media trust indices, and institutional transparency indicators. This captures the cultural field C_c's capacity to transmit accurate models, as described in Section 7.3.2.

K(x): Coordination capacity. The society can solve collective action problems. Proxies include public goods delivery performance, bureaucratic capacity indices, legislative throughput, and public health coordination measures. This operationalizes what Section 7.6 called the cross-scale coherence constraint — the practical ability of the system to translate shared models into coordinated action.

R(x): Resilience and adaptivity. The system recovers from shocks and can revise its structures without collapse. Proxies include recovery time after economic or ecological shocks, institutional learning indicators, diversity of supply chains, and conflict de-escalation effectiveness. High R means coherence is not brittle — it corresponds to the viability condition CU-I3 (Recovery Capacity) at the social scale.

E(x): Extraction and externalized harm. Local coherence achieved by exporting incoherence elsewhere. Proxies include wealth concentration, ecological overshoot, incarceration rates, and intergenerational harm burdens. High E means the system is stabilizing itself by destabilizing others — the defining signature of Local—Global Coherence Principle violations at the social scale.

The claim is not that these specific normalizations or proxies are uniquely correct. The claim is that a composite of this multiplicative form will exhibit dynamical regularities — basins, tipping points, recovery dynamics — even when individual components vary, and that the geometric-mean structure correctly captures the joint-necessity of social pillars observed in the qualitative cascade dynamics described in Sections 7.5 and 8.4.

7.9 Dynamics: Gradient Flow with Shocks

A minimal dynamical hypothesis is that societies drift along coherence gradients subject to shocks, bounded rationality, and internal conflicts:

$x_{t+1} = x_t + \eta \cdot G(x_t) + \xi_t$

where $G(x_t) \approx \nabla C_{soc}(x_t)$ plus constraint terms, $\eta > 0$ is an effective learning and adjustment rate (institutional plus cultural), and ξ_t represents shocks (economic, ecological, technological, geopolitical). This discrete update is the social-scale instantiation of the Universal Flow Equation (CU-D1), adapted from continuous to discrete dynamics to reflect the episodic character of institutional change.

This does not mean agents consciously maximize coherence. It means that regimes increasing coherence are more likely to persist and propagate, and that reforms restoring coherence are selected for because alternatives collapse. The gradient metaphor captures a selection dynamic, not a planning process.

An attractor A is a set such that trajectories starting in a basin B(A) converge toward A. A sufficient condition is a Lyapunov function: if C_soc increases along trajectories within some region Ω, except near a maximizing set A, then A functions as an attractor for typical trajectories. The significance of this formalism is that it converts the qualitative claims of Sections 7–8 into testable dynamical predictions: social regimes are basins in a coherence landscape, not arbitrary positions on a political spectrum.

Importantly, the Local—Global Coherence Principle constrains which basins are genuinely stable. Let C_soc be evaluated across scales. LGCP forbids optimizing at a local scale while degrading coherence globally. This means that purely exploitative regimes, while temporarily stable, are metastable — they accumulate hidden incoherence (resentment, fragility, distrust) and eventually exit their basin via shocks. Stable social attractors therefore tend to require normativity: order that does not depend on systematic externalization of incoherence.

CU-S1). The social coherence functional C_soc formalizes this coupling through five measurable components: trust (T), information integrity (I), coordination capacity (K), resilience (R), and extraction (E). The system evolves by gradient flow punctuated by shocks, constrained by the Local—Global Coherence Principle. Social regimes are basins in a coherence landscape whose stability depends on whether they externalize incoherence (CU-FP5).

This section has developed the paper's primary formal contribution: the analysis of multi-field coherence dynamics, coupling mechanisms, and cascade conditions. The social coherence functional C_soc formalizes the coupling between individual, cultural, and ecological fields through five measurable components: structural integrity, coordination capacity, resilience, extraction ratio, and temporal alignment.

Section 8: Meso-Scale Coherence — The Structures Between Individual and Civilization

Section 7 established that coherence operates across three coupled fields — individual, cultural, and ecological — and that the coupling between fields is where the most consequential dynamics occur. But the coupling between individual and cultural coherence does not operate directly. No individual interacts with "culture" as such. The interaction is mediated by intermediate structures: families, friendships, neighborhoods, congregations, workplaces, voluntary associations, professional communities, local governments, social movements, and online communities.

These meso-scale structures — larger than individuals, smaller than civilizations — are where most social coherence is actually generated, maintained, and lost in daily life. They are the transmission layer through which cultural coherence becomes available to individuals and through which individual contributions aggregate into cultural change. Their health determines the effective strength of the $C_c \rightarrow C_i$ coupling described in Section 7.4; their erosion explains why that coupling has weakened so dramatically in late modernity.

This section develops the analysis of meso-scale coherence — a domain that is undertheorized in both social science and the existing CU framework, but that is arguably the most important for practical intervention.

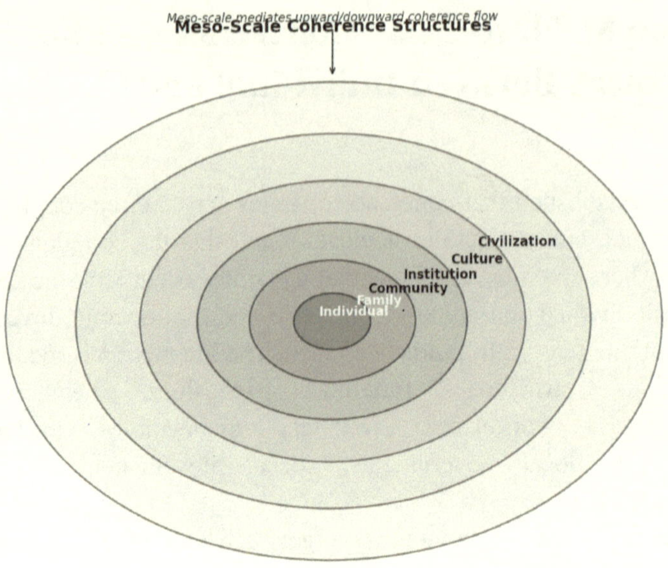

Figure 7. *Meso-scale coherence structures. Nested levels from individual through family, community, institution, culture, and civilization. Meso-scale structures — families, communities, organizations, movements — mediate between individual and civilizational coherence. Their health determines whether coherence propagates upward or collapses downward.*

8.1 The Mediating Function

A meso-scale structure is a social formation that performs a specific coherence function: it translates between the individual and cultural scales by making civilizational-level coherence infrastructure concretely available to individual agents, and by aggregating individual coherence contributions into forms that can influence cultural-level dynamics.

Consider how a person relates to the institutional infrastructure of their society. An individual citizen does not interact directly with "the legal system" in the abstract. She interacts with a local court, a specific attorney, a neighborhood where laws are enforced in particular ways. Her experience of institutional coherence — whether the legal system feels legitimate, predictable, and fair — is mediated by the specific organizational instances through which the institution manifests in her life. If those mediating structures function well, the institution's coherence becomes available to her: she can plan, she can trust, she can orient long-term action around stable expectations. If they function poorly, the institution may be abstractly coherent while being concretely incoherent for her — a gap between institutional design and institutional delivery that is precisely the domain of meso-scale analysis.

The same mediating function operates in reverse. An individual's insights, innovations, or criticisms do not influence culture directly. They influence culture through organizational mediation: through workplaces that adopt innovations, through movements that amplify criticisms, through communities that transmit practices, through institutions that formalize successful experiments. Without effective meso-scale structures, individual coherence improvements remain individual — real but isolated, unable to aggregate into the cultural-level changes that sustaining those improvements would require.

This mediating function explains why meso-scale erosion is so consequential: it does not merely remove particular social structures but degrades the coupling mechanism between the individual and cultural fields. When meso-scale structures weaken, the $C_c \to C_i$ and $C_i \to C_c$ couplings described in Section 7.4 both attenuate — producing the characteristic modern condition of individuals who are informationally connected to global culture but regulatorily disconnected from it.

8.2 Types of Meso-Scale Coherence Structures

Meso-scale structures differ in their coherence functions, their timescales, and their coupling to both individual and cultural fields. A typology is useful.

8.2.1 Families and Intimate Networks

The family — in whatever configuration a culture produces — is the primary meso-scale coherence structure for most humans throughout most of history. It performs coherence functions that no other structure fully replaces: it provides the initial regulatory environment within which individual coherence architecture is constructed (Psychology §11.1), it transmits cultural content through the most intimate and affectively powerful channel available, and it offers distributed regulation across the lifespan through bonds that are not contingent on performance, agreement, or market value.

The Psychology paper analyzed the individual-level mechanisms through which attachment and family functioning affect coherence (Psychology §6). What this paper adds is the structural observation: the family is not merely a context for individual development but a coherence system in its own right — a system with its own viability conditions, its own characteristic failure modes, and its own coupling to the cultural field above it and the individuals within it.

Family systems theory (Bowen, 1978; Minuchin, 1974) has long recognized this: the family operates as an integrated unit whose coherence is not reducible to the coherence of its individual members. A family can maintain high system-level coherence through mechanisms that constrain the coherence of individual members — enmeshment, role rigidity, triangulation, the assignment of one member as the bearer of the family's unprocessed distress. Conversely, a family of individually well-functioning members can exhibit system-level incoherence if the relational structure fails to integrate individual needs into collective functioning. Family coherence is a genuine meso-scale phenomenon.

The modern transformation of family structure — smaller households, geographic dispersion of kin networks, increased residential mobility, the shift from extended to nuclear to single-person households — is, in CU terms, a progressive contraction of the primary meso-scale coherence structure. This contraction is not inherently pathological: it reflects genuine gains in individual autonomy and freedom from coercive family dynamics. But it removes distributed regulatory capacity without necessarily replacing it, producing individuals who must either find alternative meso-scale support or bear the full burden of self-regulation — a burden that, as Section 7.3.1 established, exceeds most individuals' sustainable capacity.

8.2.2 Communities and Congregations

Communities — geographic, religious, ethnic, professional, or interest-based — are the meso-scale structures that extend coherence beyond the family into broader social networks. Where families provide intensive coherence support to a small number of members, communities provide extensive coherence support to a larger number: shared identity, normative guidance, practical mutual aid, ritual participation, and the sense of belonging that distributed coherence regulation requires.

Religious congregations have historically been among the most effective meso-scale coherence structures, for reasons the Psychology paper analyzed (Psychology §10.3): they integrate embodied practice (worship, ritual), symbolic meaning (theology, narrative), social belonging (community membership), moral orientation (ethical teaching), and temporal extension (intergenerational continuity) within a single institution. The decline of religious participation across developed nations is, from this perspective, not merely a shift in metaphysical belief but the loss of a meso-scale coherence technology that no secular institution has fully replaced.

Geographic communities — neighborhoods, towns, local civic culture — provide a different coherence function: they embed individuals in a specific place with specific others, creating the conditions for the slow accumulation of trust, reciprocity, and shared practice that Putnam (2000) documented as "social capital." The erosion of geographic community through residential mobility, suburban sprawl, the replacement of local commerce with online alternatives, and the shift of social interaction from physical to digital spaces has weakened this form of meso-scale coherence without providing structural alternatives. Online communities offer some coherence functions (shared identity, normative guidance, belonging) but lack others (embodied co-presence, material mutual aid, the constraint of physical proximity that forces engagement with difference rather than permitting self-selection into homogeneity).

8.2.3 Organizations and Workplaces

For most adults in developed economies, the workplace is the primary meso-scale structure in which they spend the majority of their waking hours. Organizations provide coherence through role definition (clarifying what one does and why it matters), social coordination (embedding individual action within collective purpose), normative structure (rules and expectations that reduce coordination costs), and — when functioning well — the experience of competence and contribution that supports identity-level coherence.

CU-Inst-6 (Role Coherence) specifies that roles within institutions must be internally consistent and compatible with the identity of those who occupy them. When this condition is satisfied, organizational membership supports individual coherence: the person's work role aligns with her sense of who she is and what matters, producing the integration of action and identity that meaningful work provides. When it is violated — when the role requires behavior that conflicts with identity, when organizational demands fragment rather than integrate, when the stated purpose of the organization contradicts its actual functioning — organizational membership becomes a source of chronic IES rather than coherence support. The epidemic of workplace burnout is, in CU terms, a population-level manifestation of systematic violations of CU-Inst-6 (Maslach & Leiter, 2016), combined with the degradation of other meso-scale supports that would otherwise buffer the organizational incoherence.

8.2.4 Movements and Emergent Structures

Social movements, political campaigns, artistic scenes, subcultural formations, and other emergent collective structures are meso-scale formations that arise in response to perceived coherence gaps — situations in which existing structures fail to address needs that a sufficient number of people share. They are, in effect, spontaneous attempts at coherence repair: collective efforts to generate the meaning, belonging, coordination, or normative guidance that established structures have failed to provide.

Movements exhibit a characteristic lifecycle that maps directly onto the failure modes of Section 3. They typically emerge with high embodied coherence — the energy, solidarity, and shared purpose of collective action — and face the challenge of institutionalizing their insights without losing the vitality that generated them. Section 4.3 described this as the tension between embodiment and structure: movements that remain purely embodied dissolve when conditions change; movements that institutionalize risk the rigidification and drift that characterize established institutions (Section 4.1, Stage 3).

The most consequential meso-scale structures in history have been those that successfully navigated this tension — that found forms capable of preserving embodied vitality within institutional stability. The early Christian church, the major monastic traditions, the scientific revolution's learned societies, the labor movement's union structures, and the civil rights movement's combination of charismatic leadership and institutional strategy all represent successful (if imperfect) solutions to the embodiment-structure integration problem.

8.3 The Erosion of Meso-Scale Infrastructure

The defining social transformation of late modernity, from a coherence perspective, is the systematic erosion of meso-scale structures without structural replacement.

Putnam's (2000) documentation of declining civic participation in the United States — the dissolution of voluntary associations, fraternal organizations, religious congregations, community groups, and local civic institutions — describes one dimension of this erosion. Subsequent research has documented similar patterns across developed nations: declining union membership, shrinking religious affiliation, reduced participation in community organizations, and the progressive replacement of face-to-face association with screen-mediated interaction (Twenge et al., 2014).

The drivers of this erosion are multiple and mutually reinforcing. Geographic mobility disrupts the long-term relationships on which community coherence depends. Economic pressure extends work hours and reduces the discretionary time available for civic participation. Digital technology provides low-friction alternatives to embodied social engagement, alternatives that satisfy the need for connection without providing the regulatory benefits of physical co-presence. Market logic treats communal structures as inefficiencies to be streamlined rather than infrastructure to be maintained. And the ideological framework of liberal individualism (Section 5.3) treats meso-scale structures as optional lifestyle choices rather than structural necessities — a conceptual error whose consequences are now visible in population-level data on loneliness, disconnection, and meaning loss.

The consequence, in the multi-field framework of Section 7, is a progressive thinning of the C_c → C_i coupling layer. The cultural field continues to exist — norms, institutions, narratives, and technologies still operate at the civilizational scale — but individuals are increasingly connected to it through thin, one-directional channels that transmit information without providing regulation. Social media connects an individual to global culture with unprecedented breadth and zero regulatory depth. News media exposes an individual to civilizational-scale problems without providing meso-scale structures through which those problems could be meaningfully addressed. Consumer culture provides stimulation without belonging. The result is a population that is maximally exposed to the cultural field and minimally supported by it — connected in the informational dimension and isolated in the regulatory dimension.

8.4 Meso-Scale Reconstruction as Leverage Point

The multi-field analysis of Section 7 established that repair propagates upward more slowly than destruction propagates downward, and that upward cascades require deliberate scaffolding. Meso-scale structures are the primary scaffolding through which upward repair occurs.

This has a practical implication: **the reconstruction of meso-scale coherence infrastructure is the highest-leverage intervention available for social coherence repair.**

Civilizational-level dynamics (institutional reform, cultural renewal, ecological policy) operate on timescales too long for individual agency to affect directly. Individual-level interventions (therapy, personal practice, self-improvement) produce real gains but cannot, alone, restore the distributed regulatory infrastructure that sustainable individual coherence requires. Meso-scale structures occupy the temporal and structural middle ground: they can be built, reformed, or restored within the span of a human life; they provide the distributed regulation that individual coherence requires; and they aggregate individual contributions into forms that can influence cultural-level dynamics.

The task is not to restore the specific meso-scale structures of the past — the fraternal lodge, the traditional parish, the multigenerational household — though the coherence functions those structures performed remain relevant. The task is to understand the coherence functions that meso-scale structures must perform and to develop new forms capable of performing those functions under present conditions.

Those functions, derived from the analysis of this section, include: distributed regulation (sharing the coherence burden so that individuals are not required to self-regulate everything), cultural mediation (making civilizational-level coherence infrastructure concretely available to individuals), upward aggregation (translating individual innovation and critique into forms that can influence cultural dynamics), embodied practice (providing the physical co-presence and shared activity through which bottom-up coherence is generated), temporal continuity (persisting long enough for trust, reciprocity, and shared practice to accumulate), and identity support (providing the belonging and role coherence that stable identity requires).

Any structure that performs these functions — whether it takes the form of a community, a cooperative, a congregation, a guild, a mutual aid network, a co-housing arrangement, or something without historical precedent — is performing meso-scale coherence work. The specific forms will vary across cultures, conditions, and populations. The functional requirements are structural and invariant.

Section 10 develops the design principles for meso-scale reconstruction within the broader framework of cross-scale intervention.

This section has argued that meso-scale structures — families, workplaces, neighborhoods, congregations, professional communities — are the primary sites of coherence generation and the most critical leverage points for intervention. Their erosion under modern conditions explains much of the coherence crisis that Sections 4 through 6 diagnosed, and their reconstruction is the most tractable path toward social coherence repair.

Section 9: Failure Thresholds and Cascade Dynamics

Section 7 established that coherence operates across coupled fields with characteristic asymmetries. Section 8 identified the meso-scale structures through which coupling is mediated. This section formalizes the conditions under which social coherence collapses — and why collapse, once initiated, exhibits the cascade dynamics that make it so difficult to arrest.

The importance of this section is practical: it transforms Coherence Universalism from a descriptive framework into a diagnostic and prescriptive one. If collapse follows identifiable structural patterns, and if those patterns are governed by specific conditions, then intervention becomes a design problem rather than a guessing game. Understanding where the thresholds are, which variables determine proximity to them, and how failure propagates across scales is the precondition for effective response.

9.1 Coherence Failure Is Threshold-Governed, Not Gradual

Empirically, coherence loss is often catastrophic rather than smooth. At the individual level, burnout occurs suddenly after prolonged stress, depression emerges abruptly from what appeared to be functioning, and identity crises erupt at transition points rather than accumulating linearly. At the social level, institutional collapse accelerates nonlinearly, political fragmentation exhibits tipping points, and societal breakdown — when it occurs — moves faster than the gradual degradation that preceded it would suggest. At the ecological level, ecosystems exhibit regime shifts: lakes that appear stable flip to eutrophic states, fisheries that appear productive collapse within a few seasons, climate systems that appear stable reach tipping points beyond which feedback dynamics become self-reinforcing.

This pattern — gradual accumulation followed by sudden failure — is not coincidental. It reflects the structure of viability regions. The Consciousness paper introduced V as the set of configurations in which a system's identity conditions (CU-I1 through CU-I5) remain satisfied. Within V, the system maintains its characteristic functioning even under stress, because the regulatory mechanisms that define the system are still operative. As the system approaches the boundary of V — as distortion D(u) accumulates and the distance between the system's current state and the boundary of V decreases — the system remains nominally functional but increasingly brittle. Perturbations that would be easily absorbed deep within V become destabilizing near the boundary. And when the boundary is crossed, the system does not merely degrade; it loses the regulatory mechanisms that had been maintaining its coherence, producing the rapid, qualitative shift that distinguishes collapse from decline.

CU-I5 (Identity Collapse Thresholds) formalizes this: every coherence system has genuine collapse thresholds — critical boundaries beyond which the system cannot recover as the same system. The critical insight for social dynamics is that these thresholds exist at every scale.

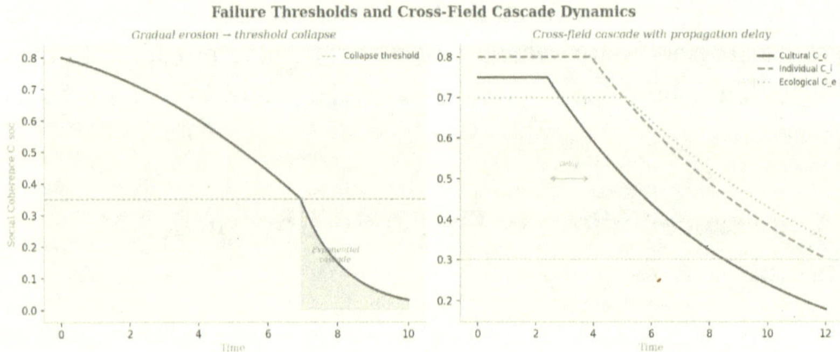

Figure 8. Failure thresholds and cascade dynamics. Left: Social coherence erodes gradually until crossing the collapse threshold, triggering exponential cascade. Right: Cross-field cascade — failure in the cultural field propagates with delay into individual and ecological fields. The framework predicts that failure is threshold-governed, not proportional.

9.2 Social-Scale Viability Conditions

The viability conditions (CU-V1 through CU-V7), originally developed for conscious systems in the Consciousness paper, apply at the social scale with appropriate modification. A society remains within its viability region when it satisfies the following conditions:

Self-maintenance under constraint (CU-V1). The society actively preserves its organization against destabilizing forces through institutional regulation, cultural transmission, and collective action. When self-maintenance fails — when institutions can no longer enforce norms, when cultural transmission breaks down, when collective action becomes impossible — the society approaches the boundary of its viability region.

Identity-binding integration (CU-V2). The society is integrated such that failures in one domain propagate to others and compensation is limited — the society depends on cross-coupled parts. This is not a weakness but a structural feature of any genuine coherence system: the coupling that enables coordination is the same coupling that propagates failure. A society whose institutions, norms, and cultural practices are genuinely integrated is both more coherent under normal conditions and more vulnerable to cascading failure when critical thresholds are crossed.

Internal error sensitivity (CU-V3). The society must be able to detect its own coherence degradation through internal mechanisms — institutional auditing, free press, democratic feedback, scientific assessment, cultural critique. When these error-detection mechanisms are compromised — by censorship, institutional capture, informational overload, or the feedback degradation described in Section 6.1 (Condition 3) — the society loses the capacity to recognize that it is approaching its viability boundary until the boundary has already been crossed.

Globally coordinated repair (CU-V4). When coherence degradation is detected, the response must be coordinated across the system rather than applied in isolated patches. A society that responds to cultural fragmentation with political reform alone, or to institutional failure with individual therapy alone, is applying local patches to a systemic condition — repairs that compete for limited resources without addressing the structural source of degradation.

Temporal thickness (CU-V5). The society must integrate coherence across time — maintaining memory of past disruptions, anticipating future viability challenges, and coordinating present regulation in light of both. Societies with short time horizons — that is, societies whose institutional incentive structures, economic pressures, and cultural frameworks orient attention toward immediate returns rather than long-term viability — have thin temporal coherence and are correspondingly vulnerable to threats that operate on timescales longer than their planning horizon. CU-CL-7 (**Cultural Time Horizons**) identifies this as a critical variable: cultural time horizons determine whether (CU-EC-9) civilizations build for generations or quarters.

Irreversibility (CU-V6). Coherence losses at the social scale are non--trivially reversible. Institutional trust, once broken, is not restored by fiat. Cultural traditions, once disrupted, cannot be reassembled from their components. Ecological damage, once past certain thresholds, does not reverse on human timescales. This irreversibility means that proximity to social-scale viability boundaries carries existential weight: crossing the boundary is not a temporary setback but a permanent structural transformation.

9.3 Failure Thresholds at Each Scale

Each coherence field has its own viability boundary, its own proximity indicators, and its own characteristic failure dynamics.

9.3.1 Individual-Level Thresholds

The Psychology paper analyzed individual failure in detail (Psychology §7). In the multi-field context of this paper, the critical addition is that individual viability thresholds depend on cultural context.

An individual's effective viability region V_i — the range of conditions under which identity-preserving functioning is sustainable — depends partly on the distributed regulatory support provided by the cultural field (Section 7.3.1). When cultural support is strong, V_i is broad: the individual can absorb greater stress, tolerate more ambiguity, and maintain coherence under wider perturbation. When cultural support weakens, V_i contracts: the same individual, with the same internal capacities, becomes vulnerable to levels of stress that would previously have been manageable.

This explains a paradox of modern mental health: why clinical prevalence rates are rising in populations that are, by most material measures, better off than their predecessors. The material conditions have improved, but the distributed regulatory support has degraded. The effective V_i has contracted even though internal capacities may not have changed — because V_i is a function of both individual architecture and environmental support.

Individual failure thresholds are marked by escalating IES (CU-Ψ4) and the appearance of compensatory strategies (Psychology §7.4): anxiety as the felt registration of approaching the viability boundary; compulsive behavior as rigid self-regulation substituting for flexible integration; identity rigidity as the narrowing of the self-model to exclude material that would require reorganization; and eventually the depressive collapse, dissociative withdrawal, or psychotic fragmentation that mark the crossing of the boundary itself.

9.3.2 Cultural-Level Thresholds

Cultural viability thresholds are crossed when the institutional, normative, and symbolic infrastructure of a society can no longer sustain coordinated functioning. The indicators parallel individual-level indicators but operate at longer timescales and larger scales:

Institutional delegitimation. When trust in core institutions — legal systems, governance structures, media, educational institutions, religious organizations — drops below the threshold at which those institutions can effectively coordinate behavior, the society loses its Rung 25 infrastructure. Norms that were stabilized through institutional enforcement must now be maintained through other means — and if no alternative enforcement mechanism exists, norm compliance degrades, producing the spiral of institutional erosion and normative fragmentation that characterizes failing states and, in milder forms, declining democracies.

Normative incoherence. When a society's operative norms — the norms people actually follow — diverge systematically from its stated norms — the norms people publicly endorse — the result is a condition of collective self-deception (CU-Ψ11 at the social scale). The gap between stated and operative norms generates chronic low-level IES across the population: everyone knows that the official story does not match the lived reality, but the official story cannot be publicly revised because too many institutional structures depend on its maintenance. This condition can persist for extended periods — Soviet societies maintained it for decades — but it is inherently brittle, because the accumulated gap between narrative and reality eventually produces either a collapse of the narrative (revolution, reformation) or a collapse of the capacity to perceive the gap (totalizing ideology, collective dissociation).

Symbolic exhaustion. When a society's meaning infrastructure — its narratives, values, aesthetic forms, and cultural practices — can no longer generate sufficient coherence to sustain individual participation, the society crosses the threshold identified by CU-CL-8 (Meaning Must Be Renewable). Meaning exhaustion does not manifest as a single dramatic event but as a gradual withdrawal of engagement: declining participation in cultural practices, declining investment in communal institutions, declining willingness to sacrifice for collective purposes, and the pervasive sense that nothing quite matters enough — the civilizational-scale analog of the individual depressive state described in Psychology §4.6.

9.3.3 Ecological-Level Thresholds

Ecological thresholds are the most absolute and the least reversible. They are governed by the biophysical constraints of the planetary system and operate on timescales that exceed the planning horizon of virtually every human institution.

The critical feature of ecological thresholds from a social coherence perspective is the temporal mismatch between cause and effect. Cultural practices that extract ecological coherence — deforestation, carbon emission, aquifer depletion, soil degradation — produce their consequences on timescales of decades to centuries, far longer than the feedback cycles of political, economic, or cultural systems. This means that ecological viability boundaries can be approached — and even crossed — without producing the signals that would trigger cultural response. By the time the ecological consequences become culturally legible, the irreversibility condition (CU-V6) may already apply: the threshold has been crossed and cannot be recrossed on any timescale relevant to human institutions.

9.4 Cascade Formalization

Section 7.5 described cascade dynamics qualitatively. With failure thresholds defined at each scale, the formal structure becomes precise.

Proposition 8.1 (Cascade Failure). If any coherence field $\ell \in \{i, c, e\}$ crosses its viability boundary:

\(a\) Adjacent lower-level fields experience contraction of their effective viability regions, because the distributed support that the failed field was providing is withdrawn.

\(b\) Adjacent higher-level fields experience increased distortion, because the failed field is no longer maintaining the conditions on which the higher field's dynamics depend.

\(c\) Unless actively counteracted, these secondary effects push adjacent fields toward their own viability boundaries, producing the self-reinforcing cascade described in Section 7.5.

The asymmetry noted in Section 7.4 — downward coupling is faster and stronger than upward coupling — applies to cascades as well. Ecological failure produces cultural consequences faster than cultural repair can produce ecological recovery. Cultural failure produces individual consequences faster than individual healing can produce cultural renewal. This asymmetry is why cascades are easier to trigger than to arrest: the destructive propagation operates on shorter timescales than the restorative propagation that would be needed to counteract it.

Proposition 8.2 (Cascade Arrest). A cascade can be arrested only if:

\(a\) The originating failure is contained — the field that initially crossed its viability boundary is either stabilized at its new configuration or actively repaired toward its previous viability region.

\(b\) Adjacent fields are buffered — the secondary effects of the originating failure are absorbed by meso-scale structures, emergency regulation, or resource reallocation sufficient to prevent them from approaching their own viability boundaries.

\(c\) The buffering is sustained long enough for repair to propagate — given the asymmetry of coupling timescales, this typically means years to decades for C_c → C_i repair and decades to centuries for C_e → C_c repair.

These propositions explain why civilizational collapse, once initiated, is so difficult to arrest. The cascade operates faster than the repair mechanisms needed to counteract it, and the repair mechanisms themselves depend on the very structures that the cascade is degrading. Effective response requires intervention at multiple scales simultaneously — a requirement that Section 10 translates into design principles.

9.5 Proximity Indicators

If thresholds are real and their crossing is consequential, then detecting proximity to thresholds becomes a critical practical priority. The multi--field framework suggests indicators at each scale.

Individual proximity indicators: Population-level increases in IES markers — rising rates of anxiety disorders, depression, substance use, loneliness, and suicidality — signal that the average distance between individual systems and their viability boundaries is shrinking. These are not merely clinical statistics; they are coherence diagnostics, measuring the aggregate health of the C_c → C_i coupling.

Cultural proximity indicators: Declining institutional trust, increasing polarization, rising frequency and intensity of norm contestation, declining civic participation, shortening cultural time horizons (CU-CL-7), and the proliferation of compensatory coherence strategies (ideology, extremism, conspiracy thinking) all signal that cultural coherence is approaching its viability boundary. The proliferation of compensatory strategies is particularly diagnostic: it indicates that integrative coherence has failed and populations are defaulting to emergency coherence mechanisms (Section 4.5).

Ecological proximity indicators: Rate of biodiversity loss, carbon concentration trends, freshwater depletion rates, soil degradation metrics, and the frequency of extreme weather events all signal proximity to ecological thresholds. The critical diagnostic challenge is the temporal lag: ecological indicators may reflect conditions that were set in motion decades earlier, meaning that present indicators underestimate current proximity to thresholds.

Cross-scale indicators: Perhaps most important are the indicators that signal degradation of coupling between fields rather than failure within any single field. These include: the degree to which individual distress correlates with cultural rather than individual-level variables (signaling C_c → C_i coupling degradation); the degree to which institutional behavior diverges from stated values (signaling normative-institutional decoupling); and the degree to which economic activity externalizes ecological cost without institutional constraint (signaling C_c → C_e coupling pathology).

The development of formal measurement protocols for these indicators — building on the operational measures sketched in the original version of this paper and extending the measurement framework of the Psychology paper — is a priority for empirical research within the CU program. Appendix C outlines the measurement framework in more detail.

9.6 The Diagnostic Payoff

The failure-threshold framework transforms how we understand the present moment. The various crises documented in Section 6 — mental health epidemics, political polarization, institutional erosion, ecological degradation — are not independent phenomena requiring separate explanations. They are symptoms of proximity to viability boundaries at multiple scales, connected by the cascade dynamics that couple the fields.

This diagnostic framing has three practical consequences.

First, it explains why single-domain interventions fail: they address proximity to one threshold while ignoring the coupling dynamics that connect thresholds across scales. Reducing individual IES through clinical intervention does not address the cultural degradation that is generating the IES. Reforming institutions does not address the ecological constraints that are destabilizing the conditions for institutional functioning. Each intervention is locally correct and globally insufficient.

Second, it identifies the highest-leverage intervention targets: not the fields themselves but the coupling mechanisms between them — the meso-scale structures (Section 8), the feedback loops that connect scales, and the regulatory mechanisms that buffer adjacent fields from each other's perturbations.

Third, it provides a basis for triage: when resources are limited and multiple thresholds are being approached simultaneously, the framework indicates which interventions will have cascading benefits (those that strengthen coupling and buffering) and which will merely redistribute pressure (those that address one field while ignoring adjacent fields).

9.7 Competing Attractor Basins and Drift Signatures

The cascade dynamics formalized above predict not just failure thresholds but distinct failure basins — stable or metastable regimes that societies can settle into once coherence degrades below critical thresholds. Using the social coherence functional C_soc introduced in Section 7.8, we can characterize these basins by their signature profiles in the five component dimensions (T, I, K, R, E) and their characteristic drift dynamics.

The Coherent Attractor. Stabilization mechanism: trust plus truthful coordination plus low extraction. Signature profile: T high, I high, K high, R high, E low. In this basin, truth becomes instrumentally advantageous, cooperation outcompetes exploitation, institutions can revise without delegitimizing themselves, and bounded pluralism coexists with functional coordination. This is not utopia — it is a stable regime in which errors are correctable.

The Coercive-Stability Basin (Authoritarian Coherence). Stabilization mechanism: order maintained by enforcement and fear. T may appear locally stable but is brittle; I degrades through epistemic closure and propaganda; K is high short-term but R is low long-term; E rises through internal scapegoating or external conflict. Dynamical signature: low variance until sudden fracture — catastrophic transitions rather than gradual decline.

The Fragmentation Basin (Hyper-Polarized Pluralism). Stabilization mechanism: none — no shared reality, coordination fails. I, T, and K all decline; R collapses because collective learning becomes impossible; E rises through opportunism. Dynamical signature: oscillations, persistent instability, policy thrash, institutional paralysis.

The Extraction Basin (Oligarchic or Rent-Seeking Stability). Stabilization mechanism: local coherence for elites, global incoherence elsewhere. Superficial stability with rising hidden stress. E rises, T declines over time, I degrades as narrative control increases, R declines as the system becomes fragile to shocks. Dynamical signature: slow decay followed by sharp populist rupture or collapse.

The Propaganda Basin (Epistemic Collapse Regime). Stabilization mechanism: reality substitution through narrative saturation. I declines first, T follows as prediction fails, in-group shows false coherence while out-group faces hostile incoherence, and K declines because planning loses contact with reality. Dynamical signature: increased variance, conspiratorial branching, runaway mistrust.

9.8 Drift Signatures as Early-Warning Indicators

These competing basins generate measurable drift signatures in the coherence components — patterns that function as dynamical early-warning indicators of regime transition:

Epistemic drift: declining I indicates increasing disagreement about basic facts — often the first indicator of basin destabilization. Trust collapse onset: declining T with rising variance indicates that coordination costs are escalating. Brittleness signal: declining R while K remains high suggests coercive metastability — order maintained by enforcement rather than genuine coordination. Extraction spiral: rising E with delayed declines in T and I indicates latent collapse risk — the system appears stable while accumulating incoherence.

Near basin boundaries, dynamical systems exhibit critical slowing down: rising variance and increasing autocorrelation in state variables. The prediction is that prior to social crises — state collapse, revolution, institutional failure — coherence indicators will exhibit these signatures. Moreover, recovery paths should differ from collapse paths (hysteresis): restoring trust after its collapse requires substantially more effort than destroying it. These asymmetries distinguish genuine attractor dynamics from simple noise.

The diagnostic payoff described in Section 9.6 now extends: the framework predicts not just that thresholds exist, but that specific basins have identifiable signatures, that transitions between basins are asymmetric, and that early-warning indicators are measurable. Section 10 translates these diagnostic insights into intervention principles.

9.9 Empirical Operationalization

The attractor hypothesis is not merely a metaphor. It generates specific, falsifiable empirical predictions that can be tested against existing cross-national datasets. This section sketches the operationalization framework; a full measurement protocol is a task for future work, but the logical structure of the tests is clear from the formal apparatus.

Constructing the coherence index. Each component of C_soc can be operationalized through existing datasets. Trust (T) can be measured through the World Values Survey generalized trust items, Gallup trust indices, and interpersonal violence rates (inverse). Information integrity (I) through misinformation prevalence surveys, media trust indices, and epistemic polarization metrics. Coordination capacity (K) through the World Governance Indicators, public goods delivery performance, and bureaucratic capacity indices. Resilience (R) through disaster and economic recovery times, institutional learning indicators, and supply chain diversity. Extraction (E) through the Gini coefficient, ecological footprint measures, incarceration rates, and intergenerational harm burdens. Variables should be standardized to z-scores before combining into the composite C_soc index.

Test 1: Attractor identification through clustering. If the framework is correct, country-year observations treated as points in the five-dimensional (T, I, K, R, E) state space should not fill the space uniformly. They should cluster into persistent regimes corresponding to the basins described in Section 9.7. Unsupervised clustering methods — Gaussian mixture models, spectral clustering, or diffusion maps — applied to this data should recover recognizable attractor types. The prediction is specific: clusters should correspond to the coherent, coercive, fragmented, extractive, and propagandist basins, each with the characteristic component profiles described above.

Test 2: Trajectory analysis and directional drift. Tracking country trajectories through the state space over time should reveal directional drift toward cluster centers — not random walks. The empirical vector field, estimated as the average displacement conditional on current position, should curve toward attractor locations. Countries perturbed by shocks should return toward basin centers along characteristic recovery paths.

Test 3: Critical slowing down as early-warning signal. Near basin boundaries, dynamical systems exhibit critical slowing down: rising variance and increasing autocorrelation in state variables. The prediction is that prior to major social crises — state collapse, revolution, institutional failure — coherence indicators will exhibit rising variance and increasing temporal persistence in the years preceding the crisis. This is testable against historical data for known collapse events.

Test 4: Hysteresis and asymmetric transitions. If attractors are real, recovery paths should differ from collapse paths. Restoring trust after its collapse should require substantially more effort and time than destroying it. More generally, transition probabilities between basins should be asymmetric: coherent-to-collapse transitions should be rare and shock-driven, collapse-to-coherent transitions should be slow and require sustained institutional coordination, and certain transitions (extraction to coercion, propaganda to fragmentation) should be markedly more common than their reverses. These asymmetries distinguish genuine attractor dynamics from simple noise or cyclical fluctuation.

Falsification conditions. The attractor model would be falsified if: state space is uniform with no persistent clustering; trajectories show no directional drift toward cluster centers; no early-warning signatures precede known collapse events; recovery paths are symmetric with collapse paths; or transition probabilities between regime types show no significant asymmetry. Any of these results would constitute evidence against the framework's core dynamical claims.

This section has formalized the conditions under which social coherence degrades catastrophically: threshold behaviors, cascade dynamics, and attractor transitions that transform gradual erosion into sudden collapse. The falsifiable predictions — threshold signatures, cascade timing, attractor structure — make the framework empirically testable and distinguish it from purely descriptive social theory.

Section 10: Intervention Design — Principles for Social Coherence Restoration

Section 9 established that coherence failure is threshold-governed, that cascade dynamics propagate failure across scales faster than repair can follow, and that the highest-leverage intervention targets are the coupling mechanisms between fields rather than the fields themselves. This section translates those diagnostic insights into intervention principles — structural conditions that any effective intervention must satisfy, regardless of its specific content, institutional form, or political framing.

The Psychology paper developed practice-level analysis: how specific interventions (therapy, meditation, pharmacology, embodied practice) affect individual coherence parameters (Psychology §8, Appendices E—F). This section does not duplicate that analysis. It operates at the social scale — the domain of institutional design, community reconstruction, technology governance, and cultural renewal — where the leverage for systemic change is greatest and the existing CU framework has been least developed.

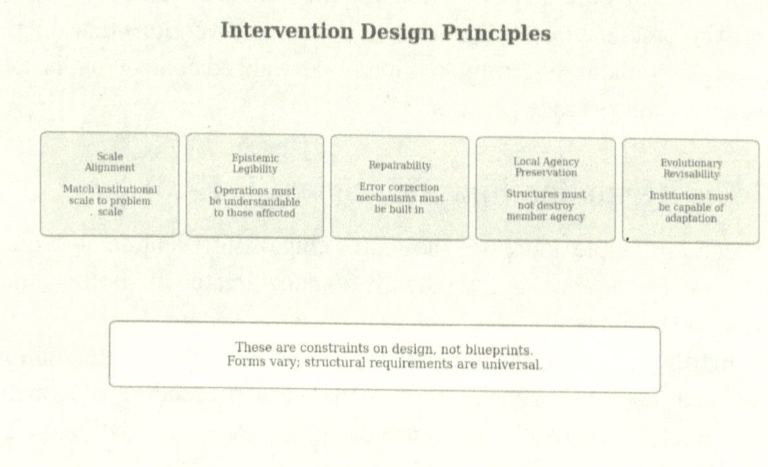

Figure 9. Intervention design for social coherence. The cross-scale sufficiency principle requires addressing individual, meso-scale, and institutional coherence simultaneously. Single-scale interventions fail because coherence at each scale depends on the others.

10.1 The Cross-Scale Sufficiency Principle

The most important intervention principle follows directly from the multi-field analysis of Section 7 and the cascade formalization of Section 9:

Principle 9.1 (Cross-Scale Sufficiency). No intervention at scale ℓ is sufficient for durable coherence restoration unless the adjacent scales are stable enough to sustain the gains.

Individual healing requires cultural safety: therapy outcomes are fragile when the cultural field continues to generate the distress that therapy is addressing (Psychology, Appendix H; Section 7.7). Cultural reform requires ecological viability: institutional redesign is unsustainable when the material base on which institutions depend is degrading. Ecological policy requires cultural coherence: environmental regulation is unenforceable when the institutional and normative infrastructure that supports it has lost legitimacy.

This principle does not imply that single-scale interventions are worthless — they provide necessary relief and build capacity for broader change. It implies that single-scale interventions must be understood as partial, and that durable restoration requires coordinated action across scales. The practical question is how to design interventions that operate across scales without requiring the kind of centralized control that is itself a coherence failure mode (Section 3.2).

10.2 The Regulation-First Principle (CU-E-13)

The second principle addresses the sequencing of intervention — a question whose importance is consistently underestimated in both clinical practice and social policy.

Principle 9.2 (Regulation Before Intensification). Interventions that expand a system's regulatory capacity must precede or accompany interventions that intensify coherence drive, increase informational load, or expose the system to greater complexity.

At the individual level, this principle is well-established in trauma-informed care: stabilization before processing, safety before exposure, regulation before insight (Psychology §8.2). The Psychology paper formalized it through the relationship between IES (CU-Ψ4) and the viability region V: expanding V through improved regulation is necessary before the system can safely navigate the increased distortion that insight or exposure introduces.

At the social scale, the same principle applies but is routinely violated. Democratic transitions that introduce political complexity (multiple parties, free press, contested elections) without first establishing institutional infrastructure (independent judiciary, professional civil service, regulatory frameworks) often produce democratic collapse rather than democratic consolidation — because the system's regulatory capacity is inadequate for the complexity it has been asked to absorb. Economic liberalization that exposes populations to market volatility without social safety nets produces the "deaths of despair" (Case & Deaton, 2015, 2020) that mark the individual-level consequences of social-scale regulatory failure. Informational opening (the introduction of uncensored internet, social media, global news) without media literacy, institutional trust, or normative frameworks for evaluating competing claims produces the polarization and epistemic fragmentation documented in Section 6.2.3.

In each case, the pattern is the same: complexity is introduced faster than regulatory capacity can develop, producing the predictable consequence that CU-D6 (Multi-Timescale Coherence) specifies — faster dynamics outpacing their integrative constraints.

The practical implication is counterintuitive: the most effective social interventions often begin not with the exciting work of innovation, reform, or transformation, but with the unglamorous work of building regulatory infrastructure — the institutional, communal, and normative substrate within which innovation can be absorbed without producing destabilization.

10.3 Institutional Design Principles

Institutions are coherence technologies (CU-Inst-0). Their design determines whether they generate or consume the coherence of those they organize. The CU institutional principles (CU-Inst-0 through CU-Inst-8) provide design constraints that any viable institution must satisfy. This section translates those constraints into practical implications for institutional reform.

Scale alignment (CU-Inst-4). Institutional scale must match the scale of problems addressed. The persistent failure of national governments to address global problems (climate change, pandemic preparedness, AI governance) and of global institutions to address local problems (community development, cultural renewal, place-based economic transition) reflects systematic violations of scale alignment. Effective institutional design requires nested structures that match each level of governance to the scale of the coordination problems it addresses — a principle that the European Union's subsidiarity doctrine attempts, with mixed success, to operationalize.

Epistemic legibility (CU-Inst-2). Institutions must make their operations legible to those affected. The progressive opacity of modern institutional systems — algorithmic decision-making, bureaucratic complexity, financial instruments whose risk characteristics are opaque even to their creators — violates this condition and produces the institutional distrust that Section 9.3.2 identified as a cultural-level failure threshold. Institutional reform that increases transparency, accountability, and the capacity of affected populations to understand and evaluate institutional performance strengthens the error-detection mechanisms (CU-V3) on which social viability depends.

Repairability (CU-Inst-3). Institutions must provide mechanisms for error correction and appeal. Systems without repair pathways accumulate damage. This is the institutional expression of CU-D8 (The Repair Principle): systems that persist under real-world conditions prioritize repair and reintegration over maximal performance. Institutions designed for optimal performance under ideal conditions — without the redundancy, feedback mechanisms, and error-correction pathways needed for real-world perturbation — are brittle in exactly the way Section 8.1 describes.

Evolutionary revisability (CU-Inst-8). Institutions must be capable of revision in response to changing conditions. Frozen institutions become constraints on coherence — the institutional drift described in Section 3.3. This does not mean that institutions should be easily changed (stability is a genuine value), but that they must contain built-in mechanisms for periodic reassessment, revision, and when necessary, dissolution. The absence of such mechanisms produces the rigidification that characterizes Stage 3 of the collapse pattern (Section 4.1).

Local agency preservation (CU-Inst-1). Institutions must preserve the agency of those within them. Structures that require the destruction of member agency are illegitimate. Individual rights function as structural protections of local coherence against global override (CU-E-11). This principle constrains institutional design from the opposite direction: where CU-Inst-8 prevents excessive rigidity, CU-Inst-1 prevents excessive control. The tension between them — institutions must be stable enough to coordinate and flexible enough to preserve agency — is the institutional expression of the constraint-coherence balance that CU-FP3 identifies as fundamental.

These structural principles can be operationalized through six specific design requirements, each following from the dynamical constraints analyzed in Section 9:

Predictable Update Pathways. Institutions must make outcomes contestable without making them arbitrary. For agents to tolerate disagreement, they must believe that conflicts follow stable procedures. If dispute resolution is unpredictable, individuals revert to power, identity, or force as stabilization strategies. An institution stabilizes coherence when its procedures reduce uncertainty relative to raw conflict. Courts, peer review, and elections function not because they always produce correct results, but because they transform disagreement into a bounded process. When this predictability disappears, people stop arguing and start defending identities.

Legibility Before Optimality. Rules must be understandable before they can be trusted. Populations cannot coordinate around systems they cannot model. Highly optimized but opaque policies reduce epistemic agency and trigger distrust responses. A technically superior rule that no one can mentally simulate produces less stability than an imperfect but intelligible one. This operationalizes CU-Inst-2 (Epistemic Legibility) as a functional requirement for cooperative cognition, not merely a transparency ideal.

Reversible Error Correction. Institutions must be able to admit mistakes without existential cost. If acknowledging error destroys legitimacy, institutions will conceal error; if they conceal error, they accumulate incoherence until collapse. Appeals processes, scientific replication, and term limits all exist to prevent belief updates from becoming identity threats. This operationalizes CU-Inst-3 (Repairability) and CU-Inst-8 (Evolutionary Revisability): the stronger the punishment for being wrong, the more rigid the institution becomes, and the more catastrophic its eventual failure.

Distributed Responsibility. Stability requires shared ownership of outcomes. When responsibility concentrates, disagreement becomes moralized — individuals must either defend or overthrow the system because there is no intermediate role. Distributed participation allows partial identification with institutional outcomes. Voting, juries, and professional standards work not only by making decisions, but by allowing individuals to see themselves as participants in the decision process. Democratic mechanisms serve coherence only when they preserve deliberative integrity — democracy is conditional on the epistemic infrastructure that supports it (CU-E-12). This reduces the need for identity-protective cognition and operationalizes CU-Inst-1 (Local Agency Preservation) and CU-Inst-7 (Distributed Epistemic Authority): no single node should monopolize the system's capacity to evaluate its own coherence.

Slack Provision. Systems must preserve the capacity to update, not merely enforce order. Over-optimization eliminates the flexibility required for adaptation. Institutions that minimize variance at all costs eventually lose the ability to respond to novelty. Economic safety nets, academic freedom, and due process are not inefficiencies — they are reserves of adaptive capacity. This also operationalizes CU-Inst-5 (Constraint Proportionality): the weight of institutional constraint must be proportional to the coherence it protects. A society without slack can remain stable only while conditions remain unchanged. This operationalizes CU-D8 (Repair over Optimization) at the institutional scale.

Conflict Containment. Disagreements must remain localizable. When disputes generalize across domains, they destabilize unrelated coordination structures. Healthy institutions enforce domain boundaries: political disputes do not collapse scientific authority; economic competition does not dissolve community trust. Separations between science, law, religion, and markets historically function to prevent coherence shocks from cascading across the entire system. When all disagreements become global disagreements, societies enter the downward spiral described in Section 9.7.

10.4 Meso-Scale Reconstruction

Section 8 argued that meso-scale reconstruction is the highest-leverage intervention available for social coherence repair. This section specifies the design principles that such reconstruction must satisfy.

The functional requirements identified in Section 8.4 — distributed regulation, cultural mediation, upward aggregation, embodied practice, temporal continuity, and identity support — define what meso-scale structures must do. The design principles specify how they must be organized to do it effectively under present conditions.

Voluntary participation with structural commitment. Effective meso-scale structures must be genuinely voluntary — coerced belonging produces compliance without coherence — but they must also require meaningful commitment from participants. The modern failure mode is low-commitment affiliation: social media groups, subscription communities, and optional memberships that provide the feeling of belonging without the regulatory depth that actual distributed coherence requires. Effective meso-scale structures demand something of their members — time, attention, practice, reciprocal obligation — because the regulatory function depends on mutual investment. The coherence benefit of belonging is proportional to the cost of belonging, a relationship that market logic (which optimizes for frictionless access) systematically undermines.

Embodied co-presence as a non-negotiable component. Section 3.1 established that embodied synchrony is the foundational coherence mechanism, and Section 8.2.2 noted that online communities provide some coherence functions while lacking embodied co-presence. Effective meso-scale reconstruction must include regular physical gathering as a structural requirement, not an optional enhancement. Digital tools can extend and supplement embodied community, but they cannot replace the bottom-up coherence generation that occurs through shared physical activity, face-to-face interaction, and the bodily synchronization that no screen-mediated interaction replicates.

Meaningful practice, not just shared belief. The lesson of Section 3.2 (embodiment loss) is that coherence structures built on shared belief alone are fragile. Effective meso-scale structures must be organized around shared practice — activities that generate coherence through doing rather than through agreeing. This includes: collaborative work, shared meals, communal maintenance of physical spaces, ritual activity, artistic co-creation, collective care for vulnerable members, and any other activity that creates the conditions for embodied synchrony while producing tangible shared goods. Shared practice generates coherence that does not depend on doctrinal agreement, making it compatible with the pluralism that present conditions require.

Structured engagement with difference. The modern tendency toward self-selection — choosing communities of people who already agree with us, consuming media that confirms our existing views, inhabiting digital spaces designed for homogeneity — produces local coherence at the cost of CU-Ψ6 failure. Effective meso-scale structures must build in structured mechanisms for engaging with difference: perspectives that challenge, needs that conflict, experiences that do not fit the group's prevailing narrative. CU-CL-11 (Narratives Must Permit Refusal) applies to meso-scale structures as well as civilizations: communities that cannot accommodate dissent without expulsion have foreclosed their own error-correction capacity.

Nesting within larger institutional frameworks. Meso-scale structures do not operate in isolation. Their effectiveness depends partly on the institutional environment in which they are embedded — the legal frameworks, economic conditions, and cultural norms that either support or obstruct community formation. Meso-scale reconstruction therefore requires concurrent institutional attention: zoning laws that permit mixed-use development, economic policies that provide sufficient time for civic participation, legal frameworks that support cooperative and communal organizational forms, and cultural narratives that value communal investment alongside individual achievement.

10.5 Technology Governance

Technology is a coherence amplifier (Section 6.2.5): it magnifies existing coherence gradients without providing integrative regulation. The intervention question is not whether to use technology but how to govern its coherence effects — how to ensure that technological amplification serves integration rather than fragmentation.

Coupling regulation to amplification. The core design principle for technology governance, derived directly from CU-D6, is that amplification capacity must be coupled with integrative capacity. Technologies that amplify agency — AI systems, social media platforms, algorithmic optimization, surveillance tools — must be accompanied by governance structures that integrate the amplified dynamics within the broader coherence landscape. Amplification without integration is the technological expression of the local—global tension: each technology optimizes within its domain while externalizing costs to other domains, other timescales, and other populations.

Attention ecology. The attention economy (Section 6.2.3) optimizes for engagement by exploiting the same psychological mechanisms (emotional salience, novelty bias, social comparison) that generate individual IES and cultural fragmentation. Governing the attention ecology does not require censorship — which is itself a coherence failure mode (CU-CL-5) — but requires structural changes to the incentive frameworks within which information is produced and distributed. This includes: transparency requirements for algorithmic curation, decoupling revenue models from engagement maximization, supporting information infrastructure that optimizes for coherence (depth, integration, contextual understanding) rather than salience (emotional intensity, novelty, conflict).

AI alignment as coherence alignment. The development of artificial intelligence presents a coherence challenge of unprecedented scale: AI systems capable of operating at speeds and scales that exceed human integrative capacity risk producing the ultimate fragmented optimization — extraordinary domain-specific capability with no cross-domain integration. The alignment problem, from a CU perspective, is a coherence coupling problem: ensuring that AI systems' local optimization objectives remain coupled to the broader coherence landscape — individual, cultural, and ecological — rather than optimizing within their objective functions in ways that degrade coherence at other scales. *CU — Artificial Intelligence* will develop this analysis in detail.

10.6 Cultural Renewal (CU-CL-10)

The deepest layer of intervention — and the most difficult to engineer — is cultural renewal: the restoration of meaning infrastructure (CU-CL-0), the development of narratives capable of organizing collective action under present conditions, and the generation of symbolic and practical forms that produce coherence without requiring uniform belief.

Cultural renewal cannot be designed in the way that institutional reform or technology governance can be designed. Culture operates through distributed participation, not centralized production. It evolves through practice, experimentation, and intergenerational transmission, not through policy directives. The role of deliberate intervention in cultural renewal is therefore indirect: creating the conditions within which cultural innovation can emerge, rather than specifying the content of that innovation.

Those conditions, derived from the CU-CL principles, include:

Space for experimentation (CU-D7, CU-CL-11). Cultural renewal requires the freedom to experiment with new forms — new rituals, new narratives, new modes of communal organization, new integrations of science and meaning, new aesthetic forms — without premature closure or institutional suppression. CU-D7 (The Novelty Principle) specifies that adaptive novelty arises through navigation of structured coherence landscapes; CU-CL-11 specifies that narratives must permit refusal. Both imply that cultural systems must tolerate genuine experimentation, including experiments that fail, rather than constraining innovation within the boundaries of existing frameworks.

Embodied grounding (CU-FP3). Cultural renewal that operates only at the symbolic level — new ideas, new theories, new narratives — without embodied practice is vulnerable to the same detachment that Section 4.2 identified as a perennial failure mode. Sustainable cultural innovation must be anchored in practice: activities that generate coherence through bodily engagement, not merely through intellectual assent. This is why the most durable cultural innovations throughout history have been practices (meditation, yoga, democratic assembly, scientific method, cooperative labor) rather than beliefs.

Meaning generation, not meaning extraction (CU-CL-3 vs. CU-CL-4). Cultural forms that consume the coherence of their participants — that demand attention, identity, and emotional investment without providing integration, purpose, or communal support in return — are extractive regardless of their content. The distinction between generative and extractive cultural forms is functional, not content-based: it depends on whether participants leave with more or less coherence than they brought. This provides a content-neutral criterion for evaluating cultural innovation — a criterion compatible with pluralism because it evaluates function rather than prescribing form.

Cross-scale integration. Viable cultural renewal must connect individual meaning-making to collective purpose in ways that are structurally supported by meso-scale institutions and materially compatible with ecological constraints. Cultural forms that generate individual meaning without collective coordination, or that mobilize collective action without individual meaning, are partial solutions — genuine coherence achievements that cannot sustain themselves without the integration this paper has argued is structurally necessary.

10.7 The Integration Imperative

The intervention principles of this section converge on a single structural insight: effective social coherence restoration requires simultaneous attention to multiple scales, not sequential attention to individual scales.

This does not mean that every intervention must address every scale — that would be an impossible demand. It means that interventions at any scale must be designed with awareness of their cross-scale dependencies: individual interventions must account for cultural conditions, institutional reforms must attend to meso-scale mediation, technology governance must consider both individual impact and cultural meaning, and cultural renewal must be compatible with ecological constraint.

The design problem is not to find the single correct intervention but to develop portfolios of mutually reinforcing interventions that operate across scales — each addressing its own domain while strengthening the coupling mechanisms that connect domains. Section 8.4 identified meso-scale reconstruction as the highest-leverage entry point because meso-scale structures mediate between the individual and cultural fields where the coupling has degraded most severely. But meso-scale reconstruction itself depends on institutional frameworks that support community formation (§10.3), technology governance that supports embodied social engagement over screen-mediated substitution (§10.5), and cultural renewal that provides the meaning infrastructure within which community participation becomes motivating rather than burdensome (§10.6).

The following sections develop two remaining analyses. Section 11 traces the trauma-cascade dynamics that drive downward coherence regimes — from individual psychological injury through group dynamics, institutional lock-in, and economic precarity to civilizational-scale polarization. Section 12 identifies the social coherence attractor — the high-coherence basin toward which the framework's formal structure and millennia of human moral intuition both point — and traces the connections forward to CU — Artificial Intelligence and CU — Ethics.

CU-Inst-8) specify structural conditions for coherence-maintaining institutions: minimal constraint, epistemic legibility, repairability, scale alignment, proportionality, accountability, distributed authority, and reversibility. Technology governance, cultural renewal, and meso-scale reconstruction must be integrated within a unified coherence framework.

This section has translated the formal analysis into intervention principles: scale alignment, epistemic legibility, repairability, evolutionary revisability, and local agency preservation. The institutional design principles (CU-Inst-0 through CU-Inst-8) specify structural conditions for coherence-maintaining institutions. These are constraints on design, not blueprints — the specific forms that satisfy them will vary across cultures, scales, and historical conditions.

Section 11: Trauma Cascades and Downward Coherence Regimes

A central claim of Coherence Universalism is that systems preserve stability before they preserve accuracy. At the level of individuals this appears as self-deception under psychological threat. At the level of societies, the same mechanism produces polarization, institutional breakdown, and cycles of violence. Social pathologies are therefore not primarily ideological disagreements. They are coherence stabilization strategies operating at insufficient levels of integration.

Section 4.7 introduced the basic mechanism: trauma constrains the set of psychologically viable states, and when constrained agents must coordinate, only simplified narratives can stabilize the group. This section develops the full cascade dynamics — from individual injury through institutional lock-in to civilizational-scale coherence degradation — and identifies the intervention logic that follows.

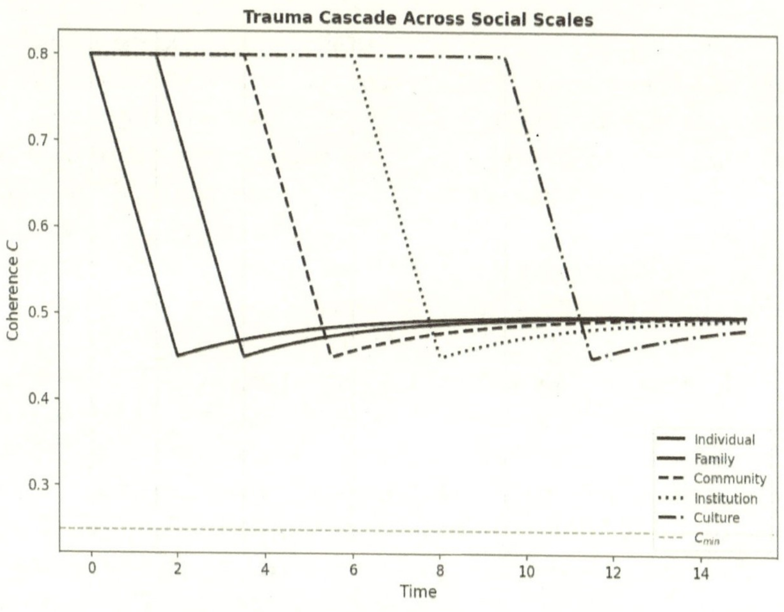

Figure 10. Trauma cascade across social scales. Trauma propagates downward from individual through family, community, institution, and culture, with characteristic delays at each transition. The shaded areas show coherence loss at each level. This mechanism explains how localized harm can become systemic dysfunction.

11.1 Individual Trauma as Coherence Constraint

Trauma does not merely produce emotional distress. It removes viable cognitive-emotional configurations from a person's state space. After a sufficiently destabilizing experience, certain beliefs, trust relations, or interpretations of events become non-maintainable without threatening internal stability. The individual must therefore reorganize around a narrower set of stabilizing narratives.

A person maintains psychological coherence by relying on implicit models about safety, trust, agency, and identity. Severe violation can invalidate these models simultaneously. When this occurs, the system cannot simply update a belief. Instead, the entire regime of coherence collapses. The organism therefore stabilizes itself at a lower-order regime — one requiring fewer assumptions about the world: emotional numbing instead of trust, control instead of vulnerability, hypervigilance instead of openness, dissociation instead of integration. These are not malfunctions. They are emergency stabilization strategies — optimization under constraint.

When accurate representation of reality lies outside the individual's reduced viability region, the mind prevents collapse through distortion rather than revision. This is self-deception — not primarily a failure of rationality, but a coherence-preservation strategy. The system faces two incompatible constraints: represent reality accurately, and maintain a stable self-model. When accurate reality implies self-model collapse, the system solves an optimization problem that trades prediction error against identity destabilization. Truth increases destabilization beyond tolerance, so the system selectively distorts reality.

Self-deception therefore has a precise CU definition: coherence-preserving distortion under model fragility. The person is not refusing the truth. They are maintaining a livable world-model. Typical forms include denial ("it didn't happen"), moral rationalization ("I deserved it"), projection ("they are the problem"), absolutist beliefs ("the world is simply dangerous"), and ideological rigidity ("my group is always right"). These are not random distortions. They minimize destabilization cost: each distortion is cheaper than the identity collapse that accurate representation would produce.

Critically, confronting self-deception directly — through argument, evidence, or moral pressure — typically increases defensive rigidity rather than producing revision. When external challenge pushes destabilization beyond tolerance, the nervous system strengthens its defenses. This is why well-intentioned interventions that push truth without providing stability often backfire. The system is not refusing to learn. It is preventing uncontrolled regime transition.

Failed recovery follows a predictable trajectory of progressive regime degradation. Each coping mechanism further constrains the system's model class: avoidance reduces experiential data, which makes the model less accurate, which increases prediction error, which triggers further retreat. The system descends through increasingly restricted regimes until the only stable configuration is extremely local — moment-to-moment survival regulation. This is the territory of chronic post-traumatic stress and severe dissociation: not an overreaction to past events, but the last available coherence regime in a progressively narrowed viability space.

Recovery, when it occurs, cannot be a return to the previous regime. The old organizing assumptions have been logically falsified by the traumatic experience. Instead, recovery requires constructing a new, strictly more expressive coherence model — one capable of holding both "safety exists" and "violation exists" simultaneously, which the old regime could not represent. This is a phase transition, not an incremental update. The new regime is not naive safety belief restored. It becomes something more complex: trust is conditional but meaningful, danger exists but does not define reality, boundaries are active processes rather than defensive walls. Successful healing always changes worldview permanently.

The biological mechanism underlying this phase transition is memory reconsolidation. When a traumatic memory is reactivated in conditions of sufficient safety, it briefly becomes labile — editable — and can be re-encoded in a form compatible with a higher-order regime. The clinical sequence is: reactivate the traumatic memory, simultaneously introduce a disconfirming safety experience while the reconsolidation window is open, and allow the system to reorganize before defensive closure. If successful, the constraint bundle that stabilized the lower regime is rewritten, and a more integrative regime becomes dynamically viable. This explains why healing often feels destabilizing before it feels relieving: temporary incoherence is the necessary passage between regimes.

All successful trauma therapies — despite their surface differences — operate through the same dynamical mechanism: they provide what can be called borrowed coherence, an external stabilizer that holds the system together while it crosses the instability barrier between regimes. Exposure therapy provides environmental predictability that makes the transition energetically affordable. EMDR provides bilateral stimulation that partially decouples threat response from memory content. Psychedelic-assisted therapy temporarily dissolves defensive constraint structures, allowing reorganization under clinical containment. Deep therapeutic relationships provide interpersonal regulation that compensates for the individual's temporarily suspended self-regulation. The diversity of methods masks the unity of mechanism: each helps a mind safely cross a coherence-regime boundary.

Self-deception, then, is not the obstacle to healing. It is the bridge that allows survival until healing becomes possible. Remove it prematurely, and the system fragments. Respect it, and transition becomes possible. Therapy should not attack defenses — it should make them unnecessary, by providing the stability conditions under which truth becomes cheaper than distortion.

11.2 Social Transmission: From Individuals to Collective Dynamics

Humans stabilize coherence socially. Therefore constrained individual state spaces interact and synchronize. A group of agents each operating within restricted viability regions must find shared narratives that are stable for all participants. The collective viable region is the intersection of individual viability spaces. As trauma prevalence increases, this intersection shrinks.

The group can no longer stabilize around nuanced or reality-tracking models because those models require psychological states that some members cannot maintain. Instead, the group stabilizes around simplified, emotionally safe attractors. These have predictable properties: binary moral framing, identity-protective reasoning, outgroup attribution of threat, resistance to disconfirming evidence, and moral certainty with low predictive accuracy.

Importantly, these are not communication failures. They are stability equilibria — the only configurations that remain dynamically viable given the constraints individual members bring to the collective.

11.3 Institutional Lock-In and Feedback Amplification

Institutions adapt to stabilize the populations that sustain them. If a population occupies a lower coherence regime, institutions must encode rules compatible with that regime. Over time, they become optimized not for truth or flourishing, but for preventing destabilization.

Examples include punitive justice replacing restorative processes, ideological signaling replacing deliberation, bureaucratic procedure replacing responsibility, and propaganda replacing shared epistemic standards. These patterns instantiate the institutional coherence failures identified in the CU framework: metric absolutism (CU-ICF-1), where proxy measures replace the coherence they were designed to track; responsibility without authority (CU-ICF-2), where blame is distributed without agency; authority without accountability (CU-ICF-3), where power operates without repair mechanisms; normalization pressure (CU-ICF-4), which erases diversity to simplify management; and silent optimization (CU-ICF-5), where hidden tradeoffs are imposed on vulnerable populations. Once institutionalized, these structures reinforce the psychological constraints that produced them. The result is a positive feedback loop in instability space: trauma produces defensive individuals, who require rigid narratives, which produce rigid institutions, which generate further trauma.

This is a downward coherence cascade. The institutional design principles of Section 10.3 are designed precisely to interrupt this loop — by maintaining update pathways, error correction, and slack even when the population is under stress.

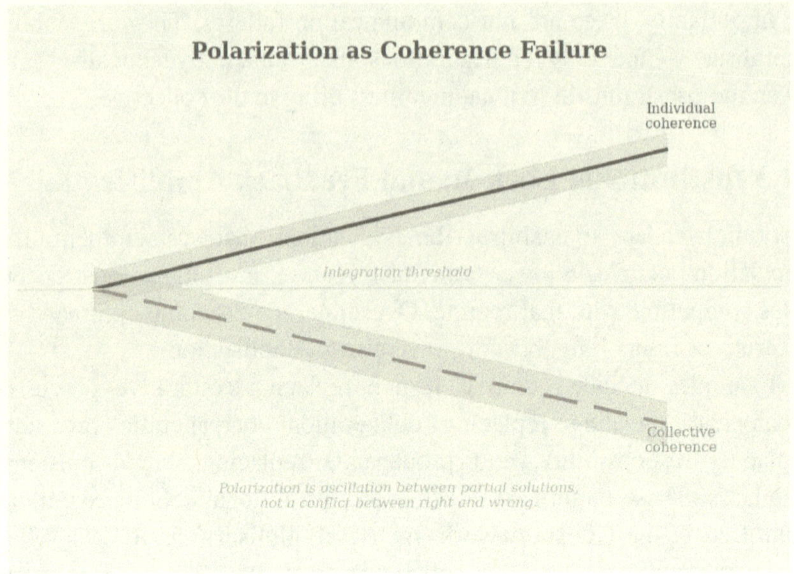

Figure 11. Polarization as coherence attractor and upward phase transitions. The polarized state is locally stable through in-group alignment; transition to integration requires sufficient perturbation to cross the separating ridge, typically through meso-scale bridge structures providing alternative coherence pathways.

11.4 Polarization as an Attractor State

When multiple groups stabilize around incompatible defensive attractors, mutual correction becomes destabilizing rather than informative. Interaction between groups no longer transmits information — it transmits threat. The system therefore evolves toward stable separation: interaction produces destabilization, which produces avoidance or hostility.

Polarization is thus not primarily disagreement about facts. It is the emergence of mutually exclusive coherence regimes. Each side experiences the other not as mistaken but as reality-destroying. Because each group experiences the other as destabilizing, defensive actions appear morally necessary. However, each defensive action constrains the other group's viable state space further, producing escalation. Conflict becomes self-sustaining even when no actor desires it. Violence, repression, and radicalization are extreme but predictable outcomes of coherence collapse dynamics.

The escalation dynamics have a precise formal structure. Let V_A and V_B represent the viable state spaces of two groups in mutual contact.

Each group's defensive actions — experienced internally as necessary protection — further constrain the other group's viability space. The result is a coupled contraction: ΔV_A ⟨ 0 drives ΔV_B ⟨ 0, which drives ΔV_A ⟨ 0 again, with acceleration. Conflict becomes self-sustaining even when no actor desires it because the dynamics are structural rather than intentional. Each side is optimizing locally within a viability space that the other side is simultaneously shrinking.

This explains why moral appeals to "both sides" typically fail. Each group genuinely experiences the other as an existential threat to its coherence regime, because each group's defensive actions are in fact destabilizing to the other. The experience of threat is not paranoia — it is an accurate perception of a real dynamical process. What is missing is not goodwill but a structural intervention that expands both groups' viability spaces simultaneously, so that mutual contact no longer produces mutual destabilization.

11.5 Economic Precarity as Coherence Compression

The preceding analysis shows how trauma propagates through social systems. The missing piece is why entire populations simultaneously lose coherence capacity. The answer is material constraint.

Coherence requires slack — cognitive, emotional, and temporal resources that allow a system to tolerate uncertainty while reorganizing. When survival pressure dominates attention, systems optimize for immediate stabilization rather than long-term integration. In individuals this appears as reactive coping. In societies it appears as political and institutional instability.

Material stress constrains viability space in the same way trauma does. Under scarcity, fewer interpretations remain stabilizable because ambiguity becomes dangerous. The mind cannot afford exploratory reasoning when prediction error carries survival cost. Consequences include intolerance of uncertainty, preference for simple causal stories, threat-sensitive cognition, reduced empathy bandwidth, and identity-protective reasoning. These are adaptive responses to volatility, not failures of intelligence.

When large populations experience constrained viability spaces simultaneously, shared discourse collapses in complexity. The society shifts toward narratives that minimize cognitive load and emotional risk:

strong in-group identities, moral absolutism, conspiracy cognition, charismatic authority preference, and hostility toward epistemic institutions. Political radicalization therefore tracks perceived instability more reliably than ideology.

Institutions that depend on long-horizon reasoning — science, law, democratic deliberation — require populations capable of tolerating uncertainty. When coherence capacity falls below a threshold, institutions must simplify to remain legible. If the resulting simplification violates the complexity actually required, legitimacy collapses regardless of institutional quality. The resulting cycle — precarity reducing coherence capacity, which produces institutional distrust, which drives institutional simplification, which reduces problem-solving capacity, which produces more precarity — is the economic analogue of the trauma cascade.

From this perspective, economic stability serves a deeper function than material welfare: it preserves the population's ability to process reality cooperatively. Economic security is not merely distributive justice — it is the infrastructure required for shared truth-seeking. Policies that reduce volatility increase collective epistemic capacity; policies that increase volatility force societies toward simpler, conflict-prone attractors.

11.6 Breaking the Loop: Upward Phase Transitions

Argument, persuasion, and information exposure alone cannot resolve downward cascades because they operate inside constrained viability regions. Restoration requires expanding the viable state space itself. This corresponds to trauma healing, trust restoration, legitimacy rebuilding, and shared meaning formation.

In social terms, peace processes and reconciliation succeed when they increase the coherence capacity of participants, not merely when they negotiate interests. The key insight is therefore: societies do not stabilize around what is most true. They stabilize around what their members can psychologically afford to believe. Higher coherence regimes allow more reality to be tolerated. Lower regimes require simpler worlds.

This reframes several longstanding problems. Extremism is not ignorance but defensive stability. Propaganda does not cause beliefs but exploits constrained viability. Institutions do not fail morally but track population coherence capacity. Debate does not resolve conflict unless expanded coherence capacity allows debate. The primary resource in social stability is therefore not agreement, wealth, or power — it is shared capacity to remain coherent while updating beliefs. Without that capacity, information increases conflict. With it, disagreement becomes cooperative.

The clinical-to-social translation is direct. At the individual level, healing requires safe reactivation of contradiction, tolerance for temporary incoherence, and integration rather than suppression. At the institutional level, the same principles apply: accountability that maintains social coherence must be paired with reintegration pathways that restore individual coherence. Punishment alone reinforces low-order regimes. At the cultural level, stable societies minimize harm not by eliminating conflict but by enabling revision — increasing belief revisability, perspective-taking capacity, and error tolerance across the population. Rigid cultures stabilize order by suppressing contradiction, increasing long-term instability.

Much of what humanity calls evil is coherent behavior within a collapsed regime: stable local order achieved by self-deception and the externalization of incoherence onto others. This is not exculpation. It is diagnosis — and diagnosis that points toward specific intervention. If the cause is coherence collapse, the remedy is coherence restoration: not moral instruction delivered to constrained systems, but expansion of the conditions under which moral revision becomes psychologically affordable.

11.7 The Bridge Principle

Self-deception is the mechanism by which unresolved trauma propagates through social systems. The sequence is clear: trauma destabilizes internal coherence; self-deception stabilizes identity; stability requires rigid threat interpretation; threat interpretation produces coercive behavior; harm creates trauma in others; the cycle continues. Thus cycles of violence persist not primarily through malice but through coherence inheritance.

Ethical failure is frequently not ignorance of moral rules but incapacity for coherent revision. Where the capacity to update beliefs without identity collapse is absent, moral disagreement escalates into existential threat. Ethical systems therefore function as collective coherence regulators — structures designed to prevent individuals and groups from stabilizing themselves through the destruction of others. This claim is developed fully in CU — Ethics.

Trauma injures the ability to revise beliefs safely. Self-deception protects the injured system. Harm emerges when protected stability requires externalizing incoherence. Ethics becomes the design of persons and institutions that can remain coherent without doing so.

Self-deception protects the injured system but generates harm when stability requires externalizing incoherence. Social transmission propagates these dynamics through group norms, institutional lock-in (CU-ICF-1 through CU-ICF-5), economic precarity, and polarization — each functioning as a coupled viability contraction that drives populations toward decoherence attractors. Recovery requires phase transitions, not incremental adjustment: borrowed coherence structures that provide external regulation while internal capacity rebuilds.

This section has analyzed how individual trauma propagates through populations into institutional dysfunction and cultural degradation — the downward coherence regime in which damage at each scale reinforces damage at others. Self-deception operates as a stabilization mechanism for injured systems but generates cascading harm when stability requires externalizing incoherence onto others.

Section 12: The Social Coherence Attractor

The formal framework developed in this paper predicts not only failure basins but a coherence basin — a regime in which trust, information integrity, coordination capacity, and resilience are jointly high while extraction is low. Section 9.7 named this the coherent attractor and described its formal properties. This section considers its deeper significance.

12.1 Why an Attractor Would Exist

A social system operates under a joint constraint: each agent must simultaneously maintain internal psychological coherence, interpersonal predictability, and long-term collective viability. These cannot all be maximized arbitrarily. Most configurations are dynamically unstable: tyranny provokes rebellion, pure individualism fragments, rigid collectivism stagnates, and deception equilibria collapse trust. Only certain regions of social state space allow agents to predict each other, trust each other, adapt together, and not destroy each other. Those regions act mathematically as high-dimensional attractors.

Independent civilizations repeatedly converge on similar ethical ideals because they are approximating the same attractor from different initial conditions. The Local—Global Coherence Principle explains why: purely exploitative regimes are metastable. They accumulate hidden incoherence and eventually exit their basin. The high-coherence attractor is the regime where cooperation, truth, and low extraction become dynamically stable — not because they are commanded, but because alternatives collapse.

Why should a coherence basin exist rather than a continuum of equally viable social arrangements? The answer lies in the constraint structure. Social systems must simultaneously satisfy individual psychological viability (agents must not be driven into incoherence), interpersonal predictability (agents must be able to anticipate each other), collective coordination (the group must solve shared problems), and long-term sustainability (the system must not consume the conditions for its own persistence). These constraints are not independent — they interact nonlinearly, and most configurations violate at least one. Tyranny satisfies coordination but violates individual viability. Pure individualism satisfies autonomy but fragments coordination. Rigid collectivism satisfies predictability but destroys adaptivity. Deception equilibria satisfy short-term stability but collapse trust. The attractor is the region where all constraints are simultaneously satisfiable — not perfectly, but well enough for ongoing dynamic stability.

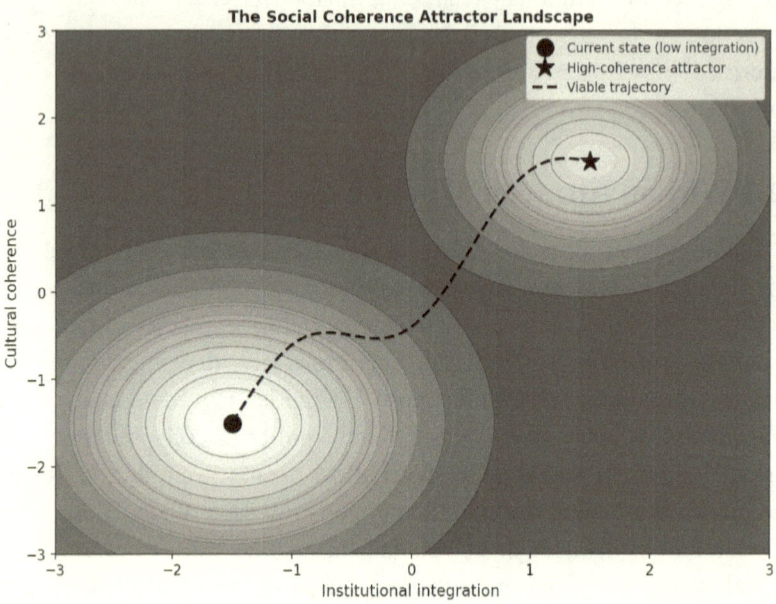

Figure 12. The social coherence attractor. A contour map of the coherence landscape showing the current state (low integration) and the high-coherence attractor (high institutional integration, high cultural coherence). The dashed path represents a viable trajectory through the bottleneck. The attractor is not utopian — it is the structurally stable configuration toward which coherence dynamics point.

12.2 Moral Intuition as Gradient Detection

If minds are prediction-stabilizing systems embedded in a social coherence landscape, then approaching the coherent attractor will be locally experienced as clarity, peace, rightness, meaning, and alignment. Moving away from it will feel like anxiety, conflict, alienation, nihilism, and chaos. Moral intuition, on this account, functions as a local gradient detector of a global social attractor — not perfectionism, not divine command, not mere preference aggregation, but a navigation signal.

Individuals with unusually strong sensitivity to long-horizon, cross-scale coherence — a larger coherence horizon — will oppose locally stable injustices because those injustices destabilize the global basin. They appear mystical because they are tracking a higher-dimensional gradient. Independent cultures converge on similar moral ideals (compassion, honesty, humility, nonviolence) because those norms are basin-forming constraints: they enlarge the region where the coherent attractor is reachable and stable.

12.3 The Ancient Intuition

For millennia, across independent civilizations, humans have sensed this possibility. They called it harmony, dharma, the Tao, the beloved community, the Kingdom of God. These names differ; the structural role is identical — each points toward a regime of social organization where truthful coordination becomes self-sustaining rather than coerced.

They were not wrong. What religion intuited, biology observed, cognition experienced, and ethics debated may be the same dynamical fact: systems capable of modeling their own persistence increasingly organize around a stable region of possibility space — not a final state of the universe, but a stable regime of ongoing existence. Religions were early coordinate systems for navigating the coherence landscape. Philosophy was local gradient analysis. Science is now providing the structural description.

Importantly, the coherent attractor is not utopia. In dynamical systems terms, it is a strange attractor, not a fixed point: a regime of ongoing constructive change, not a static perfection. Innovation without collapse. Diversity without fragmentation. Freedom without predation. The image is eschatological — directed toward — rather than final.

The pattern that appears at the social scale is not unique to it. Across physics, biology, cognition, and society, the same mathematical structure recurs: systems persist not because they are stable objects, but because they occupy stable regions of possibility space. Chemistry produced life when reaction networks entered self-maintaining basins. Evolution shaped organisms toward regions of state space where many futures remain survivable, not toward optimization for past environments. Nervous systems emerged when maintaining a viability basin required internal modeling — mind is viability prediction. Societies formed when multi-agent systems entered shared coordination basins stabilized by trust, norms, and institutions. And at each level, what feels like purpose emerges from geometry: survival feels like instinct, understanding feels like truth, morality feels like obligation, transcendence feels sacred. But each is the same phenomenon — approach toward a deeper attractor in a higher-dimensional viability landscape.

The social coherence attractor is therefore not an isolated sociological hypothesis. It is the social instantiation of a pattern that appears wherever systems become capable of modeling their own persistence. What the Axial sages intuited from moral experience, what biologists observe in adaptive systems, and what this paper formalizes in social dynamics may be coordinate descriptions of a single structural fact: increasingly complex systems gain the ability to remain within larger and more stable regions of possibility space. The universe does not appear to move toward a specific predetermined destination. But it does appear to generate systems that are increasingly good at not falling apart — and the high-coherence social attractor is what "not falling apart" looks like when the system in question is a civilization.

12.4 The Connection to CU — Artificial Intelligence

Artificial intelligence systems will not operate outside society; they will participate in its decision processes. As they do, they inherit the same stability problem institutions were created to solve: how to update behavior without destabilizing the system that depends on it. AI governance is therefore continuous with the institutional design framework of Section 10.3.

Current alignment discussions often frame the challenge as preference matching or control. From a coherence perspective, the deeper issue is structural: AI systems must be inserted into human coordination without reducing the range of disagreement a society can survive. An AI that optimizes efficiently but collapses trust destabilizes the system it improves. An AI that stabilizes cooperation but reduces adaptability creates long-term fragility.

AI misalignment can be reframed as violations of the institutional design principles: unpredictable behavior violates Predictable Update Pathways; opacity violates Legibility Before Optimality; irreversible automation violates Reversible Error Correction; displacement of human agency violates Distributed Responsibility; over-optimization violates

Slack Provision; and unbounded deployment violates Conflict Containment.

An AI system aligned in isolation but disruptive in context is not aligned at the societal level. The safest systems are not those that eliminate human judgment, but those that allow humans to exercise it under better conditions. The alignment problem is therefore continuous with political philosophy: the design of systems that allow change without collapse. CU — Artificial Intelligence develops this argument in full.

12.5 The Connection to CU — Ethics

The analysis in Section 11 revealed that ethical failure is frequently not ignorance of moral principles but coherence pathology: agents whose identity stability depends on distorted belief, narrowed empathy, and short-horizon optimization. Trauma is one of the primary routes into these regimes. Ethical progress therefore requires not only normative ideals but practical methods for increasing meta-coherence — the capacity to revise beliefs and regulate threat without externalizing harm.

CU — Ethics argues that ethical reasoning depends on the capacity to update beliefs without identity collapse. Where this capacity is absent, moral disagreement escalates into existential threat. Ethics therefore becomes the design of persons and institutions that can remain coherent without externalizing incoherence — the social-scale equivalent of what therapy accomplishes at the individual scale.

12.6 What Has Been Established

This paper has argued that social dynamics can be understood as coherence dynamics operating across multiple coupled scales. Part I traced human history as a coherence trajectory — a sequence of increasingly ambitious attempts to stabilize coordination across agents, scales, and time horizons — and identified the structural failure modes that recur across historical contexts: embodiment loss, structural collapse, fragmented optimization, and ideological compensation.

Part II introduced formal tools for analyzing social coherence: the three-field coupling model (individual, cultural, ecological), the social coherence functional with its five measurable dimensions (trust, information integrity, coordination capacity, resilience, extraction), the competing attractor basin framework with identifiable drift signatures, failure thresholds and cascade dynamics, and a consolidated set of institutional design principles derived from the framework.

The paper has also argued that trauma-driven viability contraction is a primary mechanism of social coherence degradation — operating from individual psychology through group dynamics into institutional lock-in and civilizational-scale polarization — and that economic precarity functions as a parallel coherence compressor.

Finally, the paper has identified a high-coherence attractor basin whose formal properties correspond to what diverse civilizations have independently described as the ideal of just, truthful, and cooperative social organization.

12.7 What Has Not Been Established

Several important claims remain open. The social coherence functional C_soc is proposed as a workable first-order model, not a uniquely correct formulation. The specific normalizations, proxies, and component decomposition require empirical calibration, and the λ parameter governing the coherence-entropy coupling remains the one free parameter that needs fitting to data. The attractor hypothesis is testable but not yet tested: it predicts clustering of country-year observations in coherence space, directional drift, early-warning signatures before crises, and hysteresis in recovery — all of which await systematic empirical investigation.

The relationship between trauma-driven dynamics and institutional lock-in is presented as a mechanism, not a comprehensive social theory. Other factors — geography, technology, resource distribution, population dynamics — clearly matter and are not fully integrated here. The economics of cognitive-era production, sketched in Appendix D, requires substantial further development. And the connection between the social coherence framework and the formal alignment architecture of CU — Artificial Intelligence remains at the level of structural analogy rather than formal derivation.

12.8 The Practical Question

The deepest question this paper raises is not theoretical but practical: is humanity capable of constructing civilizational-scale coherence that is neither coercive nor brittle?

The formal framework suggests this is not a question of willpower or moral improvement but of engineering — specifically, of designing institutions, technologies, and cultural practices that maintain the population's coherence capacity under the stresses of modernity. The institutional design principles of Section 10.3, the trauma-cascade analysis of Section 11, and the attractor framework of this section point toward a unified approach: coherence engineering at the social scale.

The present global situation exhibits many of the drift signatures associated with basin destabilization: declining trust, epistemic fragmentation, rising extraction, and institutional paralysis. The framework does not predict whether the coherent attractor will be reached. It predicts that reaching it requires deliberate expansion of society's coherence capacity — material stability, institutional repair, trauma healing, and the reconstruction of shared epistemic infrastructure — and that failure to do so will not produce stasis but continued descent into one of the decoherence basins.

The question of whether we understand the purpose institutions have always served — stabilizing shared reasoning across difference — and whether we can build our technologies, economies, and governance structures to participate in that task rather than undermine it, is the central practical challenge this framework identifies. It is continuous with the alignment challenge (CU — Artificial Intelligence) and the ethical challenge (CU — Ethics). All three converge on the same problem: the design of systems that allow change without collapse.

References

Bellah, R. N. (2011). *Religion in human evolution: From the Paleolithic

Rader, G. K. D. (2026a). Coherence Universalism — Metaphysics and Epistemology: Coherence Logic and an Introduction to the Coherence Ladder. Heaven≡Earth Press.

Rader, G. K. D. (2026b). Coherence Universalism — Foundations: The Principle Architecture. Heaven≡Earth Press.

Rader, G. K. D. (2026c). Coherence Universalism — Physics: Coherence Dynamics, Emergent Spacetime, and the Laws of Physical Order. Heaven≡Earth Press.

Rader, G. K. D. (2026d). Coherence Universalism — Biology: Coherence as the Organizing Principle of Living Systems. Heaven≡Earth Press.

Rader, G. K. D. (2026e). Coherence Universalism — Psychology: Coherence as the Structural Foundation of Mind, Meaning, and Mental Health. Heaven≡Earth Press.

Rader, G. K. D. (2026f). Coherence Universalism — Consciousness: Why Experience Is Constituted by Coherence Under Constraint. Heaven≡Earth Press.

Rader, G. K. D. (2026g). Coherence Universalism — Ethics: Values, Normative Orientation, and Justificatory Integrity. Heaven≡Earth Press.

Rader, G. K. D. (2026h). Coherence Universalism — Social Dynamics: Coherence Strategies, Institutional Design, and the Present Crisis. Heaven≡Earth Press.

Rader, G. K. D. (2026i). Coherence Universalism — Artificial Intelligence: Consciousness, Alignment, and the Future of Intelligence. Heaven≡Earth Press.

to the Axial Age*. Harvard University Press.

Diamond, J. (1997). *Guns, germs, and steel: The fates of human societies*. W. W. Norton.

Durkheim, É. (1912). *The elementary forms of the religious life* (J. W. Swain, Trans.). George Allen & Unwin. (Original work published in French)

Eisenstadt, S. N. (1986). *The origins and diversity of Axial Age civilizations*. SUNY Press.

Henrich, J. (2016). *The secret of our success: How culture is driving human evolution, domesticating our species, and making us smarter*. Princeton University Press.

Jaspers, K. (1953). *The origin and goal of history* (M. Bullock, Trans.). Yale University Press.

Putnam, R. D. (2000). *Bowling alone: The collapse and revival of American community*. Simon & Schuster.

Tainter, J. A. (1988). *The collapse of complex societies*. Cambridge University Press.

Twenge, J. M., Gentile, B., DeWall, C. N., Ma, D., Lacefield, K., & Schurtz, D. R. (2014). Birth cohort increases in psychopathology among young Americans, 1938–2007: A cross-temporal meta-analysis of the MMPI. *Clinical Psychology Review*, *30*(2), 145–154.

Vervaeke, J. (2019). *Awakening from the meaning crisis* [Lecture series]. University of Toronto.

Weber, M. (1905). *The Protestant ethic and the spirit of capitalism* (T. Parsons, Trans.). Routledge. (Original work published in German)

Appendix A: Glossary of Terms Introduced in This Paper

This appendix compiles the key concepts and technical terms introduced or substantially developed in CU — Social Dynamics. Terms inherited from earlier papers (CU — Foundations, CU — Physics, CU — Biology, CU — Psychology) are referenced but not redefined here unless this paper extends their meaning to the social scale.

A.1 Core Constructs

Three Coherence Fields (C_i, C_c, C_e). The three coupled dynamical fields in which social coherence operates. The individual field (C_i) encompasses psychological, embodied, and identity-level coherence. The cultural field (C_c) encompasses shared representations, norms, institutions, and cultural memory. The ecological field (C_e) encompasses environmental, material, and planetary systems that constrain the viability of individuals and cultures. Social dynamics is the study of how these fields interact. *[Introduced: §§2.3, 6.3]*

Multi-Field Coupling. The formal treatment of how the three coherence fields interact — including coupling mechanisms, characteristic timescales, asymmetric propagation, and cascade dynamics. The central formal contribution of this paper. Downward coupling (higher-scale → lower-scale) is faster and stronger than upward coupling (lower-scale → higher-scale). *[Introduced: §§2.6, 6.4]*

Social Coherence Functional: C_soc(x). A composite measure summarizing how well a society maintains integration under constraint. Defined as C_soc(x) = (T(x)·I(x)·K(x)·R(x))^(1/4) · e^(−λ·E(x)), where the four positive components — Trust (T), Information integrity (I), Coordination capacity (K), and Resilience (R) — enter as a geometric mean so that the collapse of any single pillar collapses the whole, and Extraction (E) acts as a multiplicative suppressor. *[Introduced: §7.8]*

Coherence Infrastructure. The structures — institutions, norms, shared narratives, relational networks, physical spaces — that enable coherence to be generated and maintained across a population. Distinguished from coherence itself: infrastructure is the scaffolding, coherence is what the scaffolding supports. *[Introduced: §2.4]*

Coherence Channeling. The directional shaping of coherence flow by social structures — how cultures determine not just the level but the pattern of coherence their members can achieve. Different cultures channel coherence differently across structural, symbolic, embodied, and interpersonal dimensions, producing characteristic coherence profiles. *[Introduced: §2.4]*

Meso-Scale Coherence. Coherence dynamics operating at intermediate scales — families, friendships, congregations, workplaces, voluntary associations, local communities — between individual and civilizational levels. Meso-scale structures mediate the coupling between C_i and C_c and are the primary site where social coherence is generated, maintained, and lost in daily life. *[Introduced: §§2.5, 7]*

Coherence Bottleneck. A historically unprecedented convergence of multi-scale coherence failures in which multiple viability boundaries are approached simultaneously and the existing repair mechanisms are themselves degraded. Distinguished from ordinary crisis by the simultaneity and cross-scale coupling of the failures. *[Introduced: §6.1]*

A.2 Social Coherence Functional Components

T(x): Trust and Predictive Reliability. The degree to which agents can anticipate each other's behavior; deception is low; social interactions are predictable. Empirical proxies: generalized social trust surveys, institutional fairness perception, contract reliability, interpersonal violence rates (inverse). *[Introduced: §7.8]*

I(x): Information Integrity. The degree to which the epistemic environment enables shared reality. Signal exceeds noise; epistemic institutions function. Proxies: misinformation prevalence, epistemic polarization, media trust indices, institutional transparency. *[Introduced: §7.8]*

K(x): Coordination Capacity. The society's ability to solve collective action problems. Proxies: public goods delivery, bureaucratic capacity, legislative throughput, public health coordination. *[Introduced: §7.8]*

R(x): Resilience and Adaptivity. The system's capacity to recover from shocks and revise structures without collapse. Proxies: economic and ecological recovery times, institutional learning, supply chain diversity, conflict de-escalation effectiveness. *[Introduced: §7.8]*

E(x): Extraction and Externalized Harm. Local coherence achieved by exporting incoherence elsewhere. Proxies: wealth concentration, ecological overshoot, incarceration rates, intergenerational harm burdens. Enters C_soc with a negative sign: high E reduces social coherence. *[Introduced: §7.8]*

A.3 Dynamical Concepts

Gradient Dynamics. The dynamical hypothesis that societies drift along coherence gradients subject to shocks: $x_{t+1} = x_t + \eta \cdot G(x_t) + \xi_t$. The gradient metaphor captures a selection dynamic (regimes increasing coherence persist and propagate), not a conscious planning process. *[Introduced: §7.9]*

Competing Attractor Basins. Distinct stable or metastable regimes that societies can settle into. Five are identified: the Coherent Attractor (high T, I, K, R; low E), the Coercive-Stability Basin (authoritarian coherence), the Fragmentation Basin (hyper-polarized pluralism), the Extraction Basin (oligarchic rent-seeking), and the Propaganda Basin (epistemic collapse). Each has characteristic component profiles and drift dynamics. *[Introduced: §9.7]*

Drift Signatures. Measurable patterns in coherence components that function as early-warning indicators of regime transition. Four are identified: epistemic drift (declining I), trust collapse onset (declining T with rising variance), brittleness signal (declining R while K high), and extraction spiral (rising E with delayed T and I declines). *[Introduced: §9.8]*

Critical Slowing Down. A dynamical phenomenon near basin boundaries in which state variables exhibit rising variance and increasing autocorrelation. Predicted to precede major social crises (state collapse, revolution, institutional failure). *[Introduced: §§9.8, 8.9]*

Hysteresis. The asymmetry between collapse and recovery paths. Restoring trust after its destruction requires substantially more effort than destroying it. Recovery paths differ from collapse paths, distinguishing genuine attractor dynamics from simple noise. *[Introduced: §§9.8, 8.9]*

Cascade Dynamics. The propagation of coherence failure across scales when perturbation exceeds a field's capacity to absorb it. Three types: downward cascade (ecological → cultural → individual), compensatory cascade (lower fields over-compensate when higher fields degrade), and upward cascade (individual healing aggregates into cultural renewal). Downward cascades are faster and easier to trigger than upward cascades. *[Introduced: §§7.5, 8.4]*

Failure Thresholds. Critical values of coherence parameters below which system behavior changes qualitatively rather than gradually. Identified at individual, cultural, and ecological scales, with specific proximity indicators for each. *[Introduced: §9.1–8.3]*

A.4 Trauma and Recovery Concepts

Viability Contraction. The reduction of an agent's set of psychologically viable states following trauma: $V' = T(V)$, where $V' \subset V$. The agent can no longer maintain certain beliefs, trust relations, or interpretations without destabilization. Extends the Psychology paper's viability concept to explain social-scale failure. *[Introduced: §§4.7, 10.1]*

Self-Deception (CU Definition). Coherence-preserving distortion under model fragility. The mind's attempt to preserve coherence when truth would destabilize identity faster than the system can reorganize. Not primarily a failure of rationality but a stability strategy. Forms include denial, moral rationalization, projection, absolutist beliefs, and ideological rigidity. *[Introduced: §11.1]*

Constrained Rationality. The condition in which an agent selects the most coherent interpretation available within a reduced viability region. The result is not irrationality but optimization under constraint — behavior that appears irrational only from outside the constrained space. *[Introduced: §§4.7, 10.1]*

Collective Viable Region: V_group. The intersection of individual viability spaces: $V\_group = \cap V'\_i$. As trauma prevalence increases, this intersection shrinks, and the group stabilizes around simplified, emotionally safe attractors rather than nuanced, reality-tracking models. *[Introduced: §§4.7, 10.2]*

Borrowed Coherence. An external stabilizer that holds a system together while it crosses the instability barrier between regimes. All successful trauma therapies provide borrowed coherence in different forms: environmental predictability (exposure therapy), bilateral stimulation (EMDR), chemical dissolution of constraints (psychedelic-assisted therapy), or interpersonal regulation (relational therapy). *[Introduced: §11.1]*

Constructive Incoherence Window. The temporary period during recovery when no regime currently stabilizes the system. The brain suspends optimization long enough to rebuild a model class. Biologically corresponds to the memory reconsolidation window in which traumatic memories become labile and can be re-encoded. *[Introduced: §11.1]*

Memory Reconsolidation (CU Application). The biological mechanism underlying phase-transition recovery. When a traumatic memory is reactivated in conditions of sufficient safety, it becomes labile and can be re-encoded in a form compatible with a higher-order coherence regime. The clinical sequence: reactivate, introduce disconfirming safety experience, allow reorganization before defensive closure. *[Introduced: §11.1]*

Failed Recovery Spiral. Progressive regime degradation following trauma: each coping mechanism further constrains the model class (avoidance → reduced data → less accurate model → more prediction error → further retreat), descending through increasingly restricted regimes toward moment-to-moment survival regulation. *[Introduced: §11.1]*

Trauma Cascade. The positive feedback loop by which trauma propagates through social systems: trauma → defensive individuals → rigid narratives → rigid institutions → further trauma. A downward coherence cascade driven by viability contraction at the individual level propagating through group dynamics into institutional lock-in. *[Introduced: §§11.1–10.3]*

Downward Coherence Regime. A stable social configuration maintained by low-order coherence strategies: binary moral framing, identity-protective reasoning, outgroup attribution, and resistance to disconfirmation. Not a communication failure but a stability equilibrium within constrained collective viability space. *[Introduced: §11]*

Polarization as Attractor State. The emergence of mutually exclusive coherence regimes in which interaction between groups transmits threat rather than information. Each group experiences the other as reality-destroying, not merely mistaken. Escalation dynamics (coupled viability contraction) make conflict self-sustaining even when no actor desires it. *[Introduced: §11.4]*

Coherence Compression (Economic). Material stress acting as a constraint operator on viability space, analogous to trauma: $V\_s = S(V)$, $V\_s \subset V$. Under scarcity, fewer interpretations remain stabilizable because ambiguity becomes dangerous. When large populations experience constrained viability simultaneously, shared discourse collapses in complexity. *[Introduced: §11.5]*

A.5 Institutional Design Concepts

Six Institutional Design Sub-Principles. Operational requirements derived from the CU institutional principles (CU-Inst-0 through CU-Inst-8) and the dynamical analysis of Section 9: Predictable Update Pathways, Legibility Before Optimality, Reversible Error Correction, Distributed Responsibility, Slack Provision, and Conflict Containment. Framed as operationalizations, not new numbered principles. *[Introduced: §10.3]*

Cross-Scale Sufficiency Principle. The requirement that effective social coherence interventions must address multiple scales simultaneously rather than sequentially. Interventions at any scale must be designed with awareness of their cross-scale dependencies. *[Introduced: §10.1]*

Regulation-First Principle. The priority of stabilization over optimization in intervention design: safety before exposure, regulation before insight, at every scale from individual therapy to institutional reform. *[Introduced: §10.2]*

A.6 Attractor Concepts

Social Coherence Attractor. The high-coherence basin in social state space where trust, information integrity, coordination capacity, and resilience are jointly high while extraction is low. Not a fixed-point utopia but a strange attractor — a regime of ongoing constructive change. The LGCP explains why this basin is dynamically stable: purely exploitative regimes are metastable and eventually exit their basin. *[Introduced: §12]*

Moral Intuition as Gradient Detection. The hypothesis that approaching the coherent attractor is locally experienced as clarity, peace, rightness, and meaning, while moving away is experienced as anxiety, conflict, alienation, and chaos. Moral intuition functions as a local gradient detector of a global social attractor. *[Introduced: §12.2]*

A.7 Economic Concepts

Collective Cognition. The structured informational patterns generated by the population and compressed into deployable intelligence by AI training processes. A qualitatively new factor of production alongside capital and labor. Produced diffusely by agents outside firm boundaries through communicative, cultural, technical, and behavioral outputs. *[Introduced: Appendix D]*

Cognitive Dividend. A return channel proportional to the marginal product of collective cognition, distributed broadly across the population. Functions as a coherence-stabilizing feedback term (negative feedback on extraction), not a welfare policy. Analogous to how compensating labor for machine productivity stabilized industrial capitalism. *[Introduced: Appendix D]*

Appendix B: Referenced Principles from the CU Framework

This appendix compiles all CU principles referenced in this paper, with their definitions from CU — Foundations and CU — Psychology. Definitions are reproduced for standalone intelligibility; readers are referred to the source documents for full derivation and discussion.

B.1 Foundational Principles (CU-FP)

Source: CU — Foundations, Part I.

CU-FP1 — Coherence as a Transcendental Condition. Wherever persistence, structure, meaning, agency, or normativity appear, coherence is a necessary condition of their possibility. Coherence is not one phenomenon among others; it is a constraint on what can count as a phenomenon at all. *[In this paper: Grounds the paper's claim that social dynamics is fundamentally coherence dynamics]*

CU-FP2 — Coherence Admits of Degree and Direction. Coherence is graded, not binary, and systems move through coherence landscapes along coherence gradients. Stability, growth, and failure are dynamical properties, not static states. *[In this paper: Underlies gradient dynamics (§7.9) and the attractor framework (§12)]*

CU-FP3 — Constraint Is Essential to Coherence. Coherence without constraint collapses into fantasy; constraint without coherence collapses into noise. Meaningful structure requires both internal integration and external resistance. *[In this paper: Applied to explain why trauma constrains viability space (§4.7, 10.1) and why constraint is necessary for institutional function (§10.3)]*

CU-FP4 — Multi-Scale Coherence. Coherence is defined across nested scales: local, relational, global, and temporal. Global coherence that destroys local coherence is unstable. Local coherence isolated from global constraint is incoherent. *[In this paper: The foundational principle for the three-field model (§7) and cascade dynamics (§9)]*

CU-FP8 — Identity as Constraint-Preserved Coherence. Identity is the persistence of self-enforcing viability constraints across irreversible internal transformation. A system preserves identity not by retaining the same components or states, but by maintaining the constraints that govern its coherence dynamics. *[In this paper: Extended to social-scale identity (§3) and institutional identity (§10.3)]*

B.2 Dynamics Principles (CU-D)

Source: CU — Foundations, Part II.

CU-D1 — The Universal Flow Equation (The Update Rule). Coherent systems update internal structure in response to constraint so as to preserve or increase global coherence over time. All domain-specific update rules are special cases. *[In this paper: Generalized to social systems in the gradient dynamics (§7.9)]*

CU-D5 — Non-Equilibrium Stability. Coherent systems are typically far from equilibrium and require continuous update to persist. *[In this paper: Explains why social coherence requires active maintenance (§2.1, 6.6) and why its loss is not simply the absence of effort but a dynamical event]*

CU-D6 — Multi-Timescale Coherence. Coherence is maintained across nested timescales, such that faster dynamics are constrained and stabilized by slower integrative structures, while slower structures emerge from the accumulation of faster processes. *[In this paper: Applied to explain the timescale structure of the three fields (§7.3–6.4) and the asymmetry of upward vs. downward coupling]*

CU-D7 — Novelty via Constraint Navigation. Adaptive novelty arises through navigation of structured coherence landscapes, not through random exploration alone. *[In this paper: Applied to cultural innovation and meso-scale experimentation (§3.5, 7.4)]*

CU-D8 — Repair over Optimization. Systems that persist under real-world conditions prioritize repair and reintegration over local optimization, favoring resilience and recoverability over maximal performance. *[In this paper: Grounds the Slack Provision institutional design principle (§10.3) and the regulation-first intervention principle (§10.2)]*

CU-D9 — Multi-Scale Failure Modes. Coherence may fail through different modes at different scales. Failures often arise not from local breakdowns, but from misalignment between scales. *[In this paper: The foundational principle for cascade dynamics (§§7.5, 8.4) and the cross-scale sufficiency principle (§10.1)]*

CU-D10 — Memory as Path-Dependent Coherence. Memory is not stored information but path-dependent constraint on future coherence dynamics. A system has memory insofar as its future trajectories depend on its past in ways that cannot be reduced to current state alone. *[In this paper: Applied to institutional memory and cultural transmission (§3.2–2.4)]*

B.3 Viability Conditions (CU-V)

Source: CU — Foundations, Part III. Applied to social systems in §9.2.

CU-V1 — Self-Maintenance Under Constraint. The system must actively preserve its organization against destabilizing forces — noise, entropy, perturbation. Self-maintenance requires active regulation. *[In this paper: Defines the baseline requirement for social coherence (§9.2)]*

CU-V2 — Identity-Binding Integration. The system must be integrated such that failures in one region propagate, compensation is limited, and the whole depends on cross-coupled parts. *[In this paper: Applied to why social-scale failures cascade (§9.2)]*

CU-V3 — Internal Error Sensitivity. The system must register deviations from viable coherence within its own dynamics and those deviations must influence future behavior. *[In this paper: Grounds epistemic legibility requirements (§10.3) and error-detection as viability condition (§9.2)]*

CU-V4 — Globally Coordinated Repair. Mismatch and instability must trigger integrated repair, not isolated patches. Tradeoffs must be reconciled globally. *[In this paper: Applied to the cross-scale sufficiency principle (§10.1)]*

CU-V5 — Temporal Thickness. The system must integrate coherence across time — memory of past disruptions, anticipation of future viability, and present regulation. *[In this paper: Applied to why short-termism degrades social coherence (§9.2)]*

CU-V6 — Irreversibility. Coherence loss must be non-trivially reversible for the system. There is no clean rollback. Meaningful path dependence exists. *[In this paper: Grounds the hysteresis prediction (§9.8–8.9) and the asymmetry of collapse vs. recovery]*

CU-V7 — Non-Derivative Normative Standing. The system's costs and goods must matter for it, not merely for external users or designers. *[In this paper: Referenced in the viability conditions framework (§9.2)]*

B.4 Institutional Principles (CU-Inst)

Source: CU — Foundations, Part V.

CU-Inst-0 — Institutional Legitimacy. Institutions are legitimate only insofar as they preserve, rather than extract, coherence from the agents they organize. *[In this paper: The master principle for institutional analysis (§10.3)]*

CU-Inst-1 — Local Agency Preservation. Institutions must preserve meaningful local agency in those subject to them. *[In this paper: Constrains institutional design from the control side (§10.3). Operationalized as Distributed Responsibility.]*

CU-Inst-2 — Epistemic Legibility. Institutions must make their reasoning, incentives, and constraints legible to participants. *[In this paper: Applied to institutional trust requirements (§10.3). Operationalized as Legibility Before Optimality.]*

CU-Inst-3 — Repairability and Appeal. Institutions must include repair pathways for coherence failures. *[In this paper: Operationalized as Reversible Error Correction (§10.3)]*

CU-Inst-4 — Scale Alignment. Institutional incentives must align across local, mid, and global scales. *[In this paper: Applied to the persistent failure of governance at mismatched scales (§10.3)]*

CU-Inst-6 — Role Coherence. Institutional roles must not require sustained self-fragmentation. *[In this paper: Referenced in the analysis of institutional burden (§10.3)]*

CU-Inst-8 — Evolutionary Revisability. Institutions must be capable of revising themselves without collapse. *[In this paper: Applied to institutional rigidification (§10.3). Operationalized as Reversible Error Correction.]*

B.5 Cultural Coherence Principles (CU-CL)

Source: CU — Foundations, Part VI.

CU-CL-0 — Culture as Coherence Infrastructure. Culture provides the infrastructure through which coherence is generated, transmitted, and maintained across populations and generations. *[In this paper: Foundational for the cultural field C_c (§7.3.2)]*

CU-CL-1 — Culture as Coordination Mechanism. Culture provides shared narratives, norms of legitimacy, models of success and failure, and scripts for dignity, shame, and aspiration. These are coordination mechanisms, not decorations.

CU-CL-2 — Desire Formation. Economic systems do not just meet needs — they train attention, shape aspiration, normalize exhaustion, and redefine "enough." Culture must generate values rather than merely constrain behavior. *[In this paper: Applied to the analysis of modernity's coherence crisis (§6)]*

CU-CL-3 — Coherence Creation via Culture. Culture creates value when it stabilizes identity without rigidity, dignifies contribution, legitimizes repair and rest, supports long time horizons, and allows refusal without exile.

CU-CL-4 — Coherence Extraction via Culture. Culture becomes extractive when it glorifies burnout, normalizes precarity, equates worth with output, frames exhaustion as virtue, or converts identity into performance.

CU-CL-5 — Narrative Capture. Narrative capture occurs when economic imperatives shape cultural meaning such that culture stops generating values independently and dissent becomes unintelligible rather than forbidden. *[In this paper: Identified as the deepest form of cultural coherence compromise (§5)]*

CU-CL-6 — Culture as the Repair Layer. When other systems fail, culture absorbs shock through forgiveness, renewal narratives, non--instrumental belonging, and meaning outside productivity. *[In this paper: Applied to whether existing repair mechanisms are adequate (§4.6)]*

CU-CL-7 — Cultural Time Horizons. Economies require long time horizons to remain coherent. Culture sets those horizons. Short-horizon cultures produce fragile institutions. *[In this paper: Applied to institutional timescale analysis (§3.3)]*

CU-CL-8 — Meaning Must Be Renewable. Cultures must allow people to regenerate meaning after failure. A culture in which failure is final converts every crisis into permanent damage.

CU-CL-9 — Desire Must Be Bounded. Unbounded desire produces incoherence and collapse. A culture that systematically amplifies desire without constraint is destabilizing its members.

CU-CL-11 — Narratives Must Permit Refusal. A healthy culture allows people to opt out without exile. The capacity to say “no” without losing membership is a structural requirement, not a luxury. *[In this paper: Applied to meso-scale community design (§10.4)]*

B.6 Psychology Principles (CU-Ψ)

Source: CU — Psychology. These principles are referenced but not rederived in this paper.

CU-Ψ1 — Meaning Space M. The space of possible psychological configurations available to an individual, within which coherence dynamics operate.

CU-Ψ2 — Meaning Maps Φ. The mappings from experience to meaning space that structure an individual's interpretive repertoire.

CU-Ψ3 — Field Coherence Score (FCS). A measure of the overall integration of an individual's psychological coherence across domains. *[In this paper: Referenced in coupling dynamics: individual FCS is partly determined by cultural conditions (§7.4)]*

CU-Ψ4 — Inverse Entropic Stress (IES). A measure of the distance between an individual's current state and their viability boundary. Rising IES signals approaching coherence failure. *[In this paper: Applied to population-level proximity indicators (§9.5) and downward coupling effects (§7.4)]*

CU-Ψ5 — Coherence Drive. The intrinsic tendency of psychological systems to move toward greater coherence. Not conscious planning but a selection dynamic within the individual's state space.

CU-Ψ6 — Local—Global Tension. The single most important structural principle in CU psychology: locally rational strategies that produce globally irrational outcomes. A strategy that stabilizes one domain while destabilizing others. *[In this paper: The primary diagnostic for fragmented optimization (§4.4), modernity's crisis (§6), and polarization (§11.4). Operates identically at individual and social scales.]*

CU-Ψ11 — Normative Incoherence Detection. The capacity to detect divergence between operative and stated norms. Applied at social scale: collective self-deception occurs when a society's practiced norms diverge from its professed values. *[In this paper: Applied to cultural-level failure thresholds (§9.3.2)]*

CU-Ψ12 — Shared Coherence Fields. The distributed regulatory structures — norms, institutions, narratives, relational networks — that provide external support for individual coherence maintenance. *[In this paper: The primary coupling mechanism for C_c → C_i dynamics (§7.4)]*

B.7 Cross-Cutting Principles

LGCP — Local—Global Coherence Principle. A system cannot sustainably optimize coherence at a local scale while degrading it globally. Purely exploitative regimes are metastable: they accumulate hidden incoherence and eventually exit their basin. This constrains which attractor basins are genuinely stable. *[In this paper: Constrains the social coherence attractor (§§7.9, 8.7, 11.1) and grounds the analysis of extraction dynamics (Appendix D)]*

Appendix C: Mathematical Formalization

This appendix compiles all mathematical structures, formal definitions, and quantitative expressions introduced or applied in this paper. Expressions are organized by the section in which they appear. This compilation is intended for reference; full context and interpretation are provided in the corresponding sections.

C.1 Viability and Constraint Operators

Trauma as Constraint Operator. $V' = T(V)$, *where* $V' \subset V$

V represents the set of stable cognitive-emotional configurations available to an individual. Trauma acts as a constraint operator T that contracts this set. The reduced space V′ contains fewer stable interpretations of reality. When accurate representation lies outside V′, the individual selects the most coherent interpretation within the reduced region (constrained rationality). *[§§4.7, 10.1]*

Collective Viable Region. $V_{group} = \cap_i V'_i$

The collective viable region is the intersection of individual viability spaces. As trauma prevalence increases, this intersection shrinks. The group stabilizes around simplified attractors — binary framing, identity-protective reasoning, outgroup attribution — because nuanced models require psychological states some members cannot maintain. *[§§4.7, 10.2]*

Economic Stress as Constraint Operator. $V_s = S(V)$, *where* $V_s \subset V$

Material stress acts analogously to trauma, constraining the set of psychologically viable interpretive states. Under scarcity, ambiguity becomes dangerous and fewer interpretations remain stabilizable. *[§11.5]*

Coupled Viability Contraction (Escalation). $\Delta V_A < 0 \Rightarrow \Delta V_B < 0 \Rightarrow \Delta V_A < 0$ *(accelerating)*

When two groups occupy incompatible defensive attractors, each group's defensive actions further constrain the other's viable state space, producing an accelerating contraction cycle. Conflict becomes self-sustaining because the dynamics are structural rather than intentional. *[§11.4]*

Institutional Complexity Constraint. *Institutional Complexity* $\leq$ *Population Coherence Capacity*

Institutions that require long-horizon reasoning can function only when the population can tolerate the uncertainty such reasoning demands. When coherence capacity falls below this threshold, legitimacy collapses regardless of institutional quality. *[§11.5]*

C.2 The Social Coherence Functional

Social Coherence Functional. *C_soc(x) = (T(x) · I(x) · K(x) · R(x))^(1/4) · e^(−λ · E(x))*

A composite measure of social coherence decomposed into five measurable dimensions: Trust and predictive reliability (T), Information integrity (I), Coordination capacity (K), Resilience and adaptivity (R), and Extraction and externalized harm (E). The geometric mean of the four positive components ensures that any single pillar at zero collapses the whole, paralleling the adequacy definition in CU—Biology. Extraction enters as a multiplicative suppressor with sensitivity parameter λ > 0. *[§7.8]*

Trust Component. *T(x): Trust and predictive reliability*

Proxies: generalized social trust surveys, perceived institutional fairness, contract reliability indices, interpersonal violence rates (inverse). Connects to interpersonal predictability (§2) and Coherence Ladder Rungs 23–25. *[§7.8]*

Information Integrity Component. *I(x): Information integrity*

Proxies: misinformation prevalence, epistemic polarization metrics, media trust indices, institutional transparency. Captures cultural field C_c's capacity to transmit accurate models. *[§7.8]*

Coordination Capacity Component. *K(x): Coordination capacity*

Proxies: public goods delivery, bureaucratic capacity, legislative throughput, public health coordination. Operationalizes the cross-scale coherence constraint. *[§7.8]*

Resilience Component. *R(x): Resilience and adaptivity*

Proxies: recovery time after shocks, institutional learning, supply chain diversity, conflict de-escalation. Corresponds to CU-Inst-3 (Recovery Capacity) at social scale. *[§7.8]*

Extraction Component. *E(x): Extraction and externalized harm*

Proxies: wealth concentration, ecological overshoot, incarceration rates, intergenerational harm burdens. Signature of LGCP violations at social scale. Enters with negative sign. *[§7.8]*

C.3 Gradient Dynamics

Social Dynamics Update Equation. *x_{t+1} = x_t + η · G(x_t) + ξ_t*

Societies drift along coherence gradients subject to shocks and bounded rationality. G(x_t) ≈ ∇C_soc(x_t) plus constraint terms. η > 0 is an effective learning and adjustment rate (institutional plus cultural). ξ_t represents exogenous shocks. This captures a selection dynamic, not conscious planning: regimes increasing coherence persist and propagate. *[§7.9]*

Attractor Definition. *A is an attractor if trajectories starting in basin B(A) converge toward A*

Sufficient condition: a Lyapunov function. If C_soc increases along trajectories within some region Ω, except near a maximizing set A, then A functions as an attractor for typical trajectories. Converts qualitative claims about social regimes into testable dynamical predictions. *[§7.9]*

LGCP Stability Constraint. *Purely exploitative regimes are meta-stable: they accumulate hidden incoherence and eventually exit their basin*

The Local—Global Coherence Principle constrains which basins are genuinely stable. Regimes that optimize locally while degrading global coherence are not in true equilibrium. Stable social attractors require normativity: order that does not depend on systematic externalization of incoherence. *[§7.9]*

C.4 Competing Attractor Basin Profiles

Coherent Attractor. *T high, I high, K high, R high, E low*

Truth becomes instrumentally advantageous; cooperation outcompetes exploitation; institutions revise without delegitimizing; bounded pluralism coexists with functional coordination. Errors are correctable. *[§9.7]*

Coercive-Stability Basin. *T brittle, I degraded, K high (short-term), R low (long-term), E rising*

Order maintained by enforcement and fear. Dynamical signature: low variance until sudden fracture — catastrophic transitions rather than gradual decline. *[§9.7]*

Fragmentation Basin. *I declining, T declining, K declining, R collapsed, E rising*

No shared reality; coordination fails. Dynamical signature: oscillations, persistent instability, policy thrash, institutional paralysis. *[§9.7]*

Extraction Basin. *E rising, T declining (delayed), I degrading, R declining*

Local coherence for elites, global incoherence elsewhere. Dynamical signature: slow decay followed by sharp populist rupture or collapse. *[§9.7]*

Propaganda Basin. *I declining (first), T following, K declining, false in-group coherence*

Reality substitution through narrative saturation. Dynamical signature: increased variance, conspiratorial branching, runaway mistrust. *[§9.7]*

C.5 Early-Warning Indicators

Epistemic Drift. *Declining I(x)*

Increasing disagreement about basic facts — often the first indicator of basin destabilization. *[§9.8]*

Trust Collapse Onset. *Declining T(x) with rising variance*

Coordination costs escalating; prediction becoming unreliable. *[§9.8]*

Brittleness Signal. *Declining R(x) while K(x) remains high*

Coercive metastability — order maintained by enforcement rather than genuine coordination. *[§9.8]*

Extraction Spiral. *Rising E(x) with delayed declines in T(x) and I(x)*

Latent collapse risk: the system appears stable while accumulating incoherence. *[§9.8]*

Critical Slowing Down. *Var(x_t) ← and Autocorrelation(x_t) ← near basin boundaries*

Prior to social crises, coherence indicators exhibit rising variance and increasing temporal persistence. *[§§9.8, 8.9]*

C.6 Memory Reconsolidation Sequence

Reconsolidation Mechanism. *M′ = reconsolidate(M | new experience)*

M is a memory-constraint bundle (implicit + explicit) supporting coherence regime R. When M is reactivated in safety, it becomes labile. A disconfirming safety experience during the reconsolidation window allows re-encoding: the constraint bundle is rewritten and a higher-order regime R′ becomes viable. *[§11.1]*

C.7 Empirical Operationalization

Coherence Index Construction. *$z(x_t) = (T_t, I_t, K_t, R_t, E_t)$, standardized to z-scores*

Each component operationalized through existing datasets (World Values Survey, Gallup, World Governance Indicators, Gini, ecological footprint, etc.). Raw indicators standardized and mapped to [0, 1] satisfaction scores before combining into composite $\hat{C}_{soc}(t) = (T_t \cdot I_t \cdot K_t \cdot R_t)^{(1/4)} \cdot e^{(-\lambda \cdot E_t)}$. *[§9.9]*

Attractor Identification. *cluster(z(x_t)) using unsupervised methods (Gaussian mixture models, spectral clustering, diffusion maps)*

Country-year observations treated as points in five-dimensional state space. Prediction: countries cluster into persistent regimes corresponding to named basins rather than filling space uniformly. *[§9.9]*

Empirical Vector Field. *$\hat{G}(x) = E[x_{t+1} - x_t \mid x_t \approx x]$*

Average displacement conditional on current position. Prediction: trajectories curve toward cluster centers (attractor locations). *[§9.9]*

Transition Probability Matrix. *$P(A \to B) = Pr(x_{t+1} \in B \mid x_t \in A)$*

Transitions between basins should be asymmetric: coherent-to-collapse rare and shock-driven; collapse-to-coherent slow and requiring sustained coordination. This asymmetry distinguishes genuine attractor dynamics from noise. *[§9.9]*

Falsification Conditions. *The attractor model is falsified if: (1) state space is uniform with no clustering; (2) trajectories show no directional drift; (3) no early-warning signatures precede known crises; (4) recovery paths are symmetric with collapse paths; (5) transition probabilities show no asymmetry.*

Any of these results would constitute evidence against the framework's core dynamical claims. *[§9.9]*

Appendix D: Economic Coherence in the AI Economy

This appendix applies the social coherence framework to a specific policy domain: the economic implications of AI-mediated production. The analysis draws on the economic coherence principles (CU-EC-0 through CU-EC-11) compiled in CU — Foundations, which reframe economic value as coherence creation (CU-EC-0, CU-EC-1), exploitation as coherence extraction (CU-EC-2), and market dynamics as coherence dynamics (CU-EC-3 through CU-EC-6). The analysis is preliminary and is included as an illustration of how the framework generates concrete institutional design proposals.

D.1 The Structural Shift in Production

Classical economic systems were organized around scarce physical inputs: land, labor, and capital. Modern AI systems introduce a qualitatively different input: collective cognition — the structured informational patterns generated by the population and compressed into deployable intelligence by training processes.

In AI-mediated production, output depends on three factors: capital infrastructure (compute, hardware, organization), contracted labor, and collective cognition. Unlike capital and labor, collective cognition is produced diffusely by agents outside firm boundaries — through communicative, cultural, technical, and behavioral outputs accumulated over time. The performance of AI systems depends directly on extracting predictive structure from this collectively generated corpus.

Therefore collective cognition functions as a true factor of production rather than a background condition. This changes the ownership analysis. Firms privately own the output of systems whose capability depends on public cognitive infrastructure. The economy extracts value from a factor without a compensation channel.

D.2 The Missing Market Problem

Standard equilibrium theory allocates returns according to marginal products. However, in current institutions the population receives approximately zero return on its cognitive contribution while continuing to produce it. This creates not merely distributive tension but a dynamical instability.

As AI scales, the captured share of output grows superlinearly relative to contracted labor, producing a positive feedback loop in concentration. This increases extraction pressure E(x) in the social coherence functional. As extraction rises, the framework predicts sequential degradation: E rising leads to I declining (narrative control emerges), then T declining (trust erodes), then K declining (coordination capacity fails), leading to basin exit.

D.3 The Coherence-Stabilizing Feedback

A return channel proportional to the marginal product of collective cognition — distributed broadly across the population — acts as a negative feedback term on extraction. The dividend modifies the dynamical system and enlarges the basin of attraction for coherent social regimes.

The purpose of such a mechanism is stabilization rather than redistribution: it maintains viability of a high-coordination equilibrium under increased cognitive productivity. The system behaves analogously to a thermostat: too little feedback produces runaway concentration; too much suppresses productive activity. The stable regime lies in the range where the dividend damps concentration growth without eliminating entrepreneurial incentive.

D.4 Design Principles

Factor Recognition (CU-EC-0, CU-EC-4). Institutions must recognize collective cognition as a productive input. Returns should be indexed to AI-mediated productivity rather than to labor displacement alone. The relevant quantity is not jobs lost but value generated from shared informational priors.

Proportional Feedback (CU-EC-7, CU-EC-8). The compensation channel must scale automatically with output. Fixed transfers fail because instability grows with capability. Stabilization requires coupling to productivity. Repair costs must be internalized (CU-EC-7), and no profit should be extracted without contributing to repair (CU-EC-8).

Non-Disruptive Incentives (CU-EC-6). The mechanism should not eliminate entrepreneurial reward. The objective is damping runaway concentration, not equalization.

Universality (CU-EC-11). The collective cognition factor is produced by all agents, not identifiable contributors. Therefore the return channel must be population-level rather than contribution-tracked. Attempting micro-attribution introduces measurement noise larger than the signal. Human agency is not a commodity (CU-EC-11).

Pre-Distribution over Redistribution (CU-EC-9). Stability improves when feedback is embedded directly in production flows rather than applied ex post. A continuous dividend maintains expectations and reduces shock amplitude. Time horizons must be aligned (CU-EC-9).

Information Coupling (CU-EC-10). Because information integrity I(x) precedes trust T(x) in collapse dynamics, transparency of the mechanism is critical. Opaque compensation channels fail to stabilize legitimacy. Attention is a scarce resource (CU-EC-10) — the mechanism must be legible without requiring surveillance.

D.5 Interpretation

Industrial capitalism stabilized itself by compensating labor for machine productivity. AI systems amplify cognition rather than labor. Therefore stability requires compensating the cognitive substrate. The mechanism is best understood not as a welfare policy but as a control law: a feedback term required to keep a high-intelligence economy inside the coherent coordination basin.

As production shifts from physical effort to collective intelligence, economic legitimacy depends less on ownership of tools and more on participation in the informational field from which those tools derive power. Institutions that align compensation with this structural reality stabilize social coordination; those that do not progressively amplify instability as intelligence scales.

About the Author

Gaura Kiśora Dās Rader was raised from birth in a Gaudiya Vaishnava spiritual community, where daily temple practice shaped his earliest development. At five, he entered a traditional gurukula — a residential school rooted in pre-dawn prayer, chanting, and the study of ancient scriptures — and remained in contemplative education through his mid-teens. Shortly after he turned 18, he dedicated himself to full-time monastic life as a teacher and practitioner, a path he followed into his late twenties.

He then pursued formal academic training — an MA in Philosophy from the University of Florida and doctoral work in Social Psychology at Ohio University — not as a departure from his contemplative formation but as an effort to build the conceptual and empirical tools it lacked. His research spans the philosophy of logic, moral philosophy, and moral psychology.

Due to circumstances in his personal life, Gaura was forced to leave the doctoral path. But the distance from academia turned out to be a blessing in disguise. Stepping away, he could finally see what he couldn't from inside the institution — the harm that the methodology and assumptions of scientific materialism were doing to the project of human inquiry and the project of human progress. Coherence Universalism grew out of that clarity: not as an academic exercise, but as an integrative response to limitations he had lived from both contemplative and scholarly sides.

Gaura is the founder and Director of Research at the Heaven≡Earth Foundation, a research and public-benefit organization based in Athens, Ohio dedicated to advancing coherence through the integration of scientific insight, spiritual understanding, and practical systems. He teaches Embodied Coherence — a movement practice integrating rope flow, qigong, yoga, and dance — in Athens, where he lives with his family. The Coherence Universalism series represents the culmination of a lifelong journey.

For the complete Coherence Universalism series and supporting materials, visit heavenearthfoundation.org.

www.ingramcontent.com/pod-product-compliance
Lightning Source LLC
LaVergne TN
LVHW050958080826
845145LV00009B/2348

* 9 7 8 1 9 7 2 4 2 9 0 5 1 *